A

SERIES of ANSWERS

TO CERTAIN

POPULAR OBJECTIONS,

AGAINST SEPARATING FROM THE

REBELLIOUS COLONIES,

AND

DISCARDING THEM ENTIRELY:

BEING THE

CONCLUDING TRACT

OF THE

DEAN OF GLOCESTER,

ON THE SUBJECT OF

AMERICAN AFFAIRS.

GLOCESTER:
PRINTED BY R. RAIKES;
AND SOLD BY
T. CADELL, IN THE STRAND, LONDON.
M.DCC.LXXVI.

First Published 1776
Reprinted 1970

LIBRARY OF CONGRESS CATALOG CARD NUMBER:
72-124798

PRINTED IN THE UNITED STATES OF AMERICA

P R E F A C E.

THE Motives, which formerly determined the Author to postpone his Animadversions on Mr. LOCKE's Theory on Government, subsist still in their full Vigour: Or rather they have of late acquired additional Strength. For most undoubtedly, cool Disquisitions and metaphysical Speculations on the Origin of civil Society, and the Nature of civil Government, would be very little attended to, if ushered into the World during the Heat of Action, and amidst the Flames of War. But nevertheless I beg Leave to observe, that tho' I have postponed the Subject, in order to introduce the ensuing

Treatise,

Treatife, which appears to be more fuit-
able to the prefent Juncture, I am far
from having abandoned my original Plan :
Having indeed made a confiderable Pro-
grefs in the Work, and intending (God
willing) to lay it before the Public, as foon
as a Pacification fhall render fuch a Subject more feafonable, than it is at prefent.
In the mean Time, I have further to obferve, that the Principles laid down in my
17th Sermon, preached on the 30th of
January [printed for RIVINGTON] is the
Foundation, which I propofe to build upon : So that the Difcerning and Judicious
may, if they pleafe, know before-hand,
whether the Foundation is folid, and firm
enough to fupport the Superftructure.

IN regard to the following Treatife, I
requeft the candid and impartial Reader
(for as to the bigoted, the uncandid, or
malevolent, I muft leave them to act as
they pleafe) to form his Judgment concerning it, not from a fingle Circumftance, or two, but from the whole Force
of the Argument, *confidered in one View.*

It

It may poffibly, nay probably be, that I may be miftaken in a few Particulars, and that I may have been impofed upon thro' a wrong Information in others ; and yet the main, grand Argument remain as firm as ever. I will not therefore be anfwerable for every minute Point, or trifling Circum-ftance ; but I hold myfelf obliged to de-fend the Truth, and Importance of the general Doctrine.

Men, who have a bad Caufe to defend, will catch at Shadows, pretending to raife mighty Triumphs on imaginary Victories, in order to divert the Attention of the Reader from the main Point. But Men, who are confcious of having Truth on their Side, will be the lefs attentive to mere Circumftantials; becaufe they know, they are right as to Effentials. I have frequently experienced this Fact; and par-ticularly in the Difpute between Dr. Franklin and myfelf : Which, as it has an intimate Connection with the enfuing Treatife, and will ferve to throw a ftrong Light on certain Manœuvres, now endea-

A 3   voured

voured to be concealed, I will lay before the Public.

At the very Time, when Dr. Frank-lin oppofed the Stamp-Act, as being un-conftitutional, and fubverfive of the Li-berties of *America*, he was by the Favour of his prefent Majefty, continued Poft-Mafter General for the Province of *Penfil-vania* :—An Office this! which, accord-ing to his own Doctrine, was created by an *unconftitutional* Act of a *tyrannical* Par-liament in the Reign of Queen Ann, and during the Adminiftration of the Whigs. However, as he could reconcile it to his Confcience to enjoy this *unconftitutional, lucrative* Place ; fo it feems, that after the Stamp Bill had paft into a Law, his Confci-ence became lefs fqueamifh in regard to that alfo, as will appear by the Sequel.

Now, in the firft and fecond Editions of my Fourth Tract, unhappily for me, I had charged him with procuring a Place for *himfelf* in the *American* Stamp-Office; whereas, alas! it proved to be not for *himfelf*, but for his *Friend*. And as

poor

poor Culprit was thus detected in an Offence of fo heinous a Nature, againft the eternal Truth and Rectitude of Things, great were the Exultations of the Doctor and his patriotic Friends. Reader, I plead guilty to the Indictment; *habes confitentem reum.* Therefore I will lay Dr. FRANKLIN's own State of the Cafe before you;---and this the rather, becaufe his republican Agents and Abettors, the Monthly Reviewers, have *dared me* to publifh his own Account; hoping, I fuppofe, that I had miflaid my Voucher.

In a Letter of his to me, dated *March* 2, 1774, are thefe identical Words:---
" Some Days after the Stamp-Act was
" paffed, to which I had given all the Op-
" pofition I could with Mr. GRENVILLE,
" I received a Note from Mr. WHEAT-
" LEY, his Secretary, [the fame WHEAT-
LEY, whofe Papers were afterwards *ftolen*, and *confeffed* to be in the Poffeffion of Dr. FRANKLIN, and whofe Nephew was in Danger of being *murdered,* for endeavouring to trace out the original Theft]
" defiring to fee me the next Morning.

A 4 " I

" I waited upon him accordingly, and
" found with him feveral other Colony-
" Agents. He acquainted us, that Mr.
" GRENVILLE was defirous to make the
" Execution of the Act as little inconve-
" nient and difagreeable to the *Americans*
" as poffible, and therefore did not think
" of fending Stamp Officers from hence;
" but wifhed to have *difcreet* and *reputa-*
" *ble* Perfons appointed in each Province,
" from among the Inhabitants, fuch as
" would be *acceptable* to them. For as
" they were to pay the Tax, he thought
" Strangers fhould not have the Emolu-
" ments. Mr. WHEATLEY therefore
" wifhed us to name for our refpective
" Colonies, informing us, that Mr.
" GRENVILLE would be obliged to us for
" pointing out to him *honeft* and *refponfible*
" Men, and would pay great Regard to our
" Nomination. By this plaufible, and ap-
" parently candid Declaration, *we were*
" *drawn in* to nominate: And I named for
" our Province Mr. HUGHES, faying at
" the fame Time, that I knew not whe-
" ther he would accept of it. I was only
                           " fure

" fure, that if he did, he would *execute*
" *the Office faithfully.* I foon after had
" Notice of his Appointment."

Now, can any Man in his Senfes really
believe, by perufing this Letter, that either Dr. FRANKLIN, or any of the Colo-
ny-Agents conceived fuch dreadful Ideas,
at that Juncture, of the *enflaving* Nature
and *horrid* Tendency of this Stamp-Act,
as have been fo artfully imputed to it?
No :—I am fure, he cannot in his Confci-
ence believe any fuch Thing. Yet the
whole Band of *Mock-Patriots*, and Repub-
lican-Zealots held this very Language in
all their Harangues both before, and fince;
reprefenting the poor Stamp-Act as a
Monfter more deftructive to the human
Race, than the moft terrible, *death-doing*
Giants in Romance. All therefore that
can be fairly and juftly concluded from the
Tenor of this Extract is, that the Colony-
Agents, after having made that Kind of
Oppofition which is *ufually made to every*
new Tax, conceived, that they had gone
far enough, and that now it was Time

to *acquiefce*, and to have recourfe to other
Meafures of a more pacific Turn.

As therefore Peace and Harmony were
again reftored, or at the worft, were very
likely to be reftored in a fhort Time ;
from whence comes the prefent Fiend
of Fury and Difcord among us ? Reader,
I will not mince the Matter, but declare
at once,—it came from the REGENCY
BILL : That fatal Bill has brought on
all the Calamities, which both *Great-Britain* and *America* have fuffered, or are
likely to fuffer in the prefent War. To
make this clearly appear, if it wants
any Illuftration, I would obferve, that it
had been the conftant Practice with the
Mock-Patriots and *Republicans,* for many
Years, to reprefent the late Princefs Dow-
ager of *Wales* in the moft odious Co-
lours, and to afperfe her Character in
almoft every Refpect : In which Endeavour they had certainly fo far fucceeded,
as to render her *extremely unpopular.*
Therefore, when the *Regency-Bill* was
to be framed, the Minifter, [Mr. GREN-
VILLE]

VILLE] thought it the moſt prudent Way to get it conſtructed in ſuch a Manner, as to *omit* her Name, and conſequently to exclude her from being Regent. This was Handle enough for wily, and machiavalian Politicians to take hold of. Conſequently, they, who had ſo lately, and ſo groſsly abuſed and inſulted, now as much flattered and cajoled her, offering all their Weight and Aſſiſtance to ſerve her in this Cauſe. The Bait took; her Name was inſerted in the *Regency-Bill*; the Stamp-Miniſter was diſmiſſed; and they of courſe ſucceeded in his Room. And then indeed, out of mere Neceſſity (for I do not believe it was their *inward* Choice) they were compelled to repeal that Stamp-Act, againſt which they had ſo long, and ſo vehemently exclaimed. But alas! Conſcious to themſelves, that they had done exceedingly wrong, they endeavoured to n ²nd the Matter, Tinker like, by making it much worſe; hoping (vainly hoping) to patch up the Breach they had made in the Conſtitution, by the *Soldering* of a declaratory Law. But the

the *Americans,* now taught to know their own Importance (a Doctrine, which they were always ready to learn) and feeling their own Strength in our Weaknefs, re-jected the Expedient with Difdain. The only Ufe, to which they put it, was to fwell their Catalogue of *pretended* Griev-ances with this additional one of an *en-flaving* declaratory Law. And to be fure, it ferved admirably well for that purpofe, but for no other. For as to any Thing elfe,—To pretend to bind the Colonies *in all Cafes whatfoever,* after having given fuch a recent Proof, that we *dared not* bind them to pay even an Halfpenny Tax on a News-Paper, was fuch an Inftance of Gafconading Folly as is hardly to be pa-rallelled. No Wonder then, that the Co-lonifts fhould firft treat it as a ridiculous Bravado; and then make ufe of it as a Weapon againft ourfelves, by putting it into their Lift of imaginary Wrongs.

THEREFORE, let Mr. BURKE (or the *admirable* and *excellent* Mr. BURKE, as Dr. PRICE ftiles him) call me *Court Vermin,*

as

as long as he pleafes ; yet as long as I can *crawl*, I will ever maintain, that the *Rock-ingham* Adminiftration were the Caufe, the *exciting* Caufe I mean, of the prefent War, and of all the Calamities derived from it.—

> *Hoc fonte derivata clades*
> *In patriam, populumque fluxit.*

Moreover if the *declaratory Law*, which en-acts, that the *Britifh* Legiflature has a Right to bind the Colonies *in all Cafes whatfoever*; is fo very bad, fo tyrannical, and detefta-ble, as Dr. PRICE, and the Rebel *Americans* now reprefent it;—I do further affert that *that* identical patriotic Adminiftration, and particularly Mr. BURKE, were the Authors of this very Law. Dr. PRICE knew, as well as any Man living, that fuch was the State of the Cafe: But he had not the In-genuity to acknowledge it. On the con-trary by inferting this among others, in his Recital of pretended Grievances, he has led the unwary Reader to fuppofe, that the declaratory Act, as well as the reft of the fad Oppreffions under which the poor *Americans* groaned, proceeded all from the fame hateful Caufe, from the fame

fame wicked, and execrable Miniftry; or
rather from Sets of fucceffive, tyrannical
Minifters, the fole Authors of all thofe
Evils, of which the Colonifts have fo loud-
ly, and according to him, fo juftly com-
plained.   Whereas the Truth is, that at
leaft one of thefe pretended galling *Ame-*
rican Chains was forged by his own dear
patriotic Friends and Favourites, the *Rock-*
ingham Adminiftration.

READER, this learned Gentleman Dr.
PRICE has wrote an elaborate Treatife on
moral Obligation: In which he lays down
Pofitions, which are fufficiently ftrict.
Compare them therefore, I befeech you,
with his own *latitudinarian* Practice, his
own *lax* Conduct and Behaviour in this
whole Affair.—As to the declaratory Law
refpecting the Colonies; againft which he
inveighs fo bitterly, as if it were the *novel*
Ofspring of a modern, wicked Adminiftration, and a corrupt Parliament; it is, [con-
fidered in itfelf, and not connected with
the Repeal of the Stamp-Act] no other
(and that likewife Dr. PRICE knew perfectly

fectly well) than a *Copy* of the declaratory Law of the 6th of G. I. refpecting *Ireland*, and the *re-enacting* of the 7th and 8th of WILLIAM III. refpecting *America:* All thefe WHIG Princes! WHIG Parliaments! And WHIG Adminiftrations!

INTRODUCTION

INTRODUCTION.

THE Proposal for separating totally from *North-America* is observed to make Converts every Day;—it being now acknowledged by thinking People of all Denominations, that there can be no Medium between legal Subjection to the supreme Legislature on the one Hand, and an absolute Separation from it on the other. To pretend to make Distinctions in this Case is idle and vain; for the Nature of Things will not admit of them.

In Fact, were Taxation and Representation so essentially connected, and so absolutely inseparable, as Mr. Lock and his Followers would make us believe;—then most certainly every Man's Consent [the Consent of every *moral* Agent of every Sex and Condition] ought to be

previously

previoufly obtained for *divefting* him, her, or
them of *any Part* of his, her, or their natural
Rights and Liberties in *any Refpect* whatever.
For indeed our *perfonal Rights* are nearer and
dearer to us, and are more effentially our own
[our own Property] than any adventitious Ac-
ceffion of Lands or Tenements, Goods or
Chattels. Nay, in Fact, without the former, it
would be impoffible either to acquire, or to enjoy the latter.

HENCE therefore it follows *a fortiori*, that the
Act of Navigation, and every other reftraining
or prohibitory Law made long ago, without
the Choice or Concurrence of the *Americans* either by themfelves or their Reprefentatives, yet
enforced by a Confifcation of Goods, an Impri-
fonment of their Perfons, and by various other
corporal Punifhments; — muft, according to
this Doctrine, be a more notorious Violation of
their natural Rights and Property, and indeed a
much *forer* Tax, than a paultry Halfpenny
Stamp laid on a News-Paper. Therefore between Separation and legal Subjection there can
be no Medium:—There is no Line to be
drawn.

THE former Treatifes, written by the Author
in Favour of a total Separation, have never
been

been attempted to be anſwered; not one capital Fact pretended to be denied;—not one Argument refuted;—not one Concluſion diſproved. Low, ſcurrilous Epithets, ſuch as *childiſh, viſionary, mercenary, mad,* &c. &c. have been the only Mode adopted for anſwering theſe Treatiſes. The Reader therefore will be at no Loſs in diſcovering the true and only Reaſon, why other Kinds of Anſwers were not given.

But it is rather ſingular, and to ſome Perſons may appear unaccountable, why ſo many of the *Americans* themſelves, and why *all* their republican Abettors here at Home, ſhould condemn this Propoſal of an amicable Separation with ſuch Aſperity of Language, as they have been known to do, and with ſuch heavy Execrations on its Author;---a Propoſal, which they cannot but confeſs, would put a total End to all their preſent Complaints, and redreſs every Grievance pretended to be impoſed upon them by *Great-Britain.*

Nevertheless, it is not difficult to find out the Cauſe of ſuch Overflowings of Malevolence. Every *American,* who is not intoxicated with the viſionary Schemes of a growing Empire, and of perſonal Grandeur, well knows, that the petty *American* States and Republics could not ſubmit

in

in any Degree of Safety, without the Affiftance
of *Great-Britain*, to defend them both from foreign and domeftic Enemies: --And that the
Expences of maintaining a Fleet and Army, of
building Fortreffes, and of fortifying Ports and
Harbours, of fupporting the Eclat of an independent Civil Government in each Province,
would be about ten Times as great as the Sum
which the Parent State fhould levy on or require
from them, by Way of contributing their Share
towards the general Defence of the Empire.
Therefore the wary *Americans* do not chufe to
part with thefe Benefits, while a Poffibility remains of perfuading the credulous *Englifh* ftil'
to continue them.

THE Republicans at Home are moft violently
incenfed againft the Author of this Propofal,
becaufe it would quafh at once all their darling
Projects of introducing fimilar Liberty-Meet-
ings, fimilar Congreffes, and fimilar Forms of
Government here in *Britain*;—and becaufe it
would cut off all Pretences for clamouring a-
gainft Government on Account of its tyrannizing
over the natural Rights and Liberties of their
dear perfecuted Brethren, the poor, innocent
Americans.

[WHILST I was writing the above, the following incendiary Paragraph, inferted in the
London

London Evening Poſt, Auguſt 1, 1776, as ſoon as the Nation was informed, that the King's Forces had obliged the Rebels to evacuate *Canada*,—was put into my Hands, as a Corroboration of what I was here advancing.

" Something muſt be done.

" Let the Merchants meet at Guildhall, fe-
" riouſly deliberate, and determine : Let
" them invite the *Lords*, and *Members* of the
" *Oppoſition* to join them : Let them make
" their Appeal to the People at large,
" and to the City of *London* in particular :
" Let them openly declare, that nothing but
" Neceſſity, and the Principle of Self-Preſerva-
" tion [Cataline's *Speech exactly, ſee his Ha-
rangue in* Salust] " induced them to take this
" important Step: And let them call themſelves,
" The Committee of Conservation." This
Language is ſo plain, that it needs no Comment. He that runs may read.

Nothing now remains, in order to finiſh this Controverſy, but to obviate certain Objections raiſed by the Crafty, ſwallowed by the Credulous, and terrible only to the Ignorant, againſt the Idea of a total Separation. And therefore, to put theſe Objections in as ſtrong a Light as poſſible, I ſhall here introduce them in the

Form

Form of Queſtions; in order that the Reader may the better judge, Whether their reſpective Anſwers, taking the whole Series together, be ſatisfactory or not.

A

SERIES of ANSWERS

TO CERTAIN

POPULAR OBJECTIONS,

AGAINST AN

ENTIRE SEPARATION

FROM THE

NORTHERN COLONIES.

OBJECTION I.

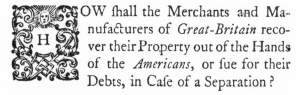 OW ſhall the Merchants and Ma-
nufacturers of *Great-Britain* reco-
ver their Property out of the Hands
of the *Americans*, or ſue for their
Debts, in Caſe of a Separation?

ANSWER I. WHILE *Great-Britain* and *Ame-*
rica remain connected together under any Form

B 4   of

of Government whatever, this Difficulty of recovering *Englijh* Property out of the Hands of
the Colonifts will never ceafe: And a total Separation is the moft effectual Cure   In Fact, thofe
Americans, who have contracted larger Debts
than they are difpofed to pay, or who want to
ftop an Importation of more Goods from the
Mother-Country, 'till their own [perhaps da-
maged] Stores are fold off at an exorbitant Profit ;—thefe Men will never ceafe to exclaim,
under one Pretence or other, againft the *Englijh* Government, as long as the Connection
fhall fubfift. Faults and Imperfections, more
or lefs, there are, and ever will be ; but it is
much eafier to caricature real Faults, and to in-
vent imaginary ones at the Diftance of 3000
Miles, than if the Scene of Action had been at
Hand. When a Separation fhall enfue, the
Faults in the *American* Government, be they
what they may, will then be all their own :
Whereas every Thing which they diflike at prefent is imputed to us ; and on this they ground
their repeated Injuries and Acts of Injuftice.

ANSWER 2. ENGLISH Creditors always found
more Trouble in fecuring or recovering their
Property in *America*, and in collecting their
Debts, than in any other Part of the Globe.
Our former Acts of Parliament, during the
Reigns

Reigns of WILLIAM III. and of GEO. I. and II. and alfo the Remonftrances of our Board of Trade, are full of Complaints on this Head.

ANSWER 3. In Cafe of a total Separation, each Colony or Province will then become in-depent, and a jealous Rival, of its Neigh-bour. No common Caufe or common Intereft will unite them together: And the Fears and Jealoufies of Trade will more effectually operate in fuch a Cafe, to enfure their Honefty and punctual Dealings, than the better Principles of Confcience and Religion. In fhort, each inde-pendent State will then be an independent rival Shop: And that Shopkeeper, who will ufe his Cuftomers beft, will infallibly get the moft Cuftom.

ANSWER 4. WERE any of thefe numerous petty States or Republics to refufe at any Time, after a proper Requifition had been made in Form, to do Juftice to the *Englifh* Merchant or Creditor, a few fmall Ships of War fent to their Coafts, not to make *Conquefts*, but *Reprifals* ac-cording to the Law of Nations, would foon teach them to be more obfervant of the Rules of Juftice and good Faith, than they are difpofed to be. And the other Provinces, their Neigh-bours and Rivals, inftead of arming in their De-fence, would rejoice at their Chaftifement.

OBJECTION

OBJECTION II.

HOW shall we prevent the *West-India* Islands from falling under the Power of the growing Empire of *America*, in Case of a Separation?

ANSWER 1. THE Northern and Southern Colonies of *America* have, and ever had, an inveterate Hatred and Antipathy against each other. And nothing prevents this from breaking out into Action * even at present, but the Apprehension of common Danger. Remove, therefore, this Apprehension, and then there will remain no central Attraction uniting them in one common League or general Association. And without such a Confederacy, it will be impossible for any one of these Republics to make the Conquest here proposed.

ANSWER 2. SHOULD two or three of these little Republics join together in such an Expedition, the rest would oppose them of Course to

---

* See the *American* Pamphlet *Plain Truth*, in Answer to *American Common Sense*.

the

the utmoft of their Power, and would invite *Great-Britain* to aid and affift them. The very Principle of Jealoufy, natural to all States, efpecially to fmall Republics, would drive them to thefe Meafures. For they would immediately fee, that the Aggrandizement of their Rivals foreboded their own Deftruction. And *Great-Britain* would at all Times be capable of holding the Balance of Power between thefe little, querulous, fretful States, by never inclining it too much to any one Side, fo as to enable it to give Law to the reft.

ANSWER 3. SUPPOSE the worft ;—fuppofe all thefe Colonies firmly united together under one Head [we know not *how*, nor *why*, nor *when*] yet even in fuch a Cafe, the paultry little Iflands in the *American* Seas would be no Object adequate to the Ambition of fuch an Empire. For after the firft Plunder was over, (and if Plunder alone was to be the Motive, it would not repay a tenth Part of the Expence of the Expedition) nothing farther could be obtained from fuch Spots without continual hard Labour, frefh Capitals, new Stocks of Slaves, a peaceable Bartering of Goods, with a long commercial Intercourfe, &c. &c. Whereas the rich and large Countries of *Mexico*, *Peru*, and the *Brazils* would be more likely Objects to roufe their Ambition,

bition, and tempt their Avarice; and they
would foon be at War with the *Spaniards* and
Portuguefe.

ANSWER 4. SUPPOSE neverthelefs, and againſt
all Probability, that the *North-Americans* not
only took Poffeffion of thefe Iflands, but alfo
kept them, and cultivated, or rather permitted,
and encouraged their *new Subjects*, the original
Proprietors or Planters to cultivate them, and
to raife Sugars, and every other *Weſt-India* Produce;—what would be the Confequence?—
Nothing but this, that the *Britiſh* Merchants
would in that Cafe buy Sugars, Rum, Ginger,
Cotton, &c. &c. juſt as they now buy Wines,
Fruit, Oils, Coffee, Chocolate, &c. &c.; that
is, at the *beſt* and *cheapeſt* Market. And it is a
Fact well known in the commercial World, that
were we permitted to enjoy the like Liberty at
prefent, we might purchafe Sugars and Rum
almoſt *Cent. per Cent.* cheaper than we now do,
by being confined to the Market of our Sugar
Planters. Moreover in that Cafe, we ſhould
probably be obliged through *Neceffity* to do *that
Juſtice*, and to make *that Reſtitution*, to a great
Part of our Fellow Creatures, which we ought
to have done long ago, by *Choice*, and through
a Principle of *mere Humanity*,—to fay nothing
of higher Motives:—That is, we ſhould teach
the

the much-injured Natives of *Africa*, which might
eafily be done, and at a fmall Expence, to cultivate their own luxuriant and fpontaneous
Sugar Canes, and to manufacture Sugars, and
feveral other Commodities, and more efpecially
Rice and Indigo, in their own native Country;
who would then exchange fuch Produce for our
European Goods and Manufactures:—Inftead
of this, we make Slaves of thefe poor Wretches,
contrary to every Principle, not only of Humanity and Juftice, but alfo of national Profit and
Advantage; as I have often proved in feveral
of my Writings both Commercial and Theolo-
gical:—We, I fay, the boafted Patrons of Liberty, and the profeffed Advocates for the natural Rights of Mankind, engage deeper in this
murderous inhuman Traffic than any Nation
whatever:—And to fhew our Confiftence, we
glory in it!

I might likewife add, that the Cane grows
fpontaneoufly in *Sicily*, where immenfe Quantities of Sugar might be made, were the *Neapo-
litan* Government to give the leaft Encouragement;—or rather, were the Court of *Naples* once
to fee its own Intereft, by removing the many
heavy Burthens, which are now laid *exprefsly*
with a View [Oh, cruel Infatuation! abfurd
Tyranny!] to check and prevent the Induftry,
Riches,

Riches, and Population of the *prolific Sicilians.*
This therefore is another ftriking Inftance of the
Pra&icability of making Sugars by Means of
common Day-Labourers and hired Servants,
without any Slaves at all.   For the Peafants of
Sicily could as well ftand the Heat of the Climate in the Culture of Canes and the Manu-
fa&ure of Sugars, as in their prefent Occupa-
tion.

Now the Advocates for Republicanifm, and
for the fuppofed Equality of Mankind, ought
to have been the foremoft in fuggefting fome
fuch humane Syftem for abolifhing the worft of
all the Species of Slavery, viz. that of the *domeftic* or *predial* Kind.   But, alas! all Republicans antient and modern, as far as Hiftory and
Experience can inform us, fuggeft no other
Schemes but thofe of pulling down and levelling all Diftin&ions above them, and of tyrannizing over thofe miferable Beings, who are unfortunately placed below them.

OBJECTION

OBJECTION III.

HOW fhall we prevent the *North-Americans* from becoming a formidable maritime Power in Cafe of a Separation?

ANSWER 1. WE may always prevent, if we pleafe, any one of thefe States from fwallowing up the reft:—In the Execution of which we fhall be fure of obtaining the Affiftance and Good-Will, and not the Execration, of the neighbouring rival States. And this Circumftance alone will prevent their becoming a formidable naval Power,

ANSWER 2. THE *American* Coafts, from *St. Auguftine* up to *Chefapeake Bay*, are generally fhallow, and not fo fit for capital Ships of War, as for fmaller Veffels from 100 to 600 Tons Burthen. This is another infuperable Bar againft *that Part* of *America* ever becoming very formidable by Sea. And as to the other Part from *Chefapeake Bay* up to *Cape Breton*, tho' there are feveral good Ports on that Coaft, yet they labour under many Inconveniences: And it may be obferved in general, that the Coafts of *Great-Britain*

Britain and *Ireland* have more than double, or
even treble, the Number of good, fafe, and
deep Harbours, and are never annoyed with Ice
or Fogs, which are to be found in all the rebellious Provinces of *North-America.*

ANSWER 3. THE Sea Coafts of *North-America*
are generally barren and unhealthy, if compared
with thofe vaft and fruitful Regions, which lie
beyond the *Alligahenny* Mountains, and ap-
proaching the Borders of the great Lakes.
Thither many of the *Americans* who dwelt near
the Sea Coafts have removed already : And the
prefent Difturbances will oblige them to do fo in
ftill greater Numbers.   New Governments and
new Common-Wealths, half civilized and half fa-
vage, will ftart up in thofe diftant Regions : For
every Topic and every Argument which the Sea
Coaft *Americans* now urge againft the Mother
Country, will be retorted with double Force a-
gainft themfelves by the *diftant* Back-Settlers.
Nay, ftrange Feuds and Animofities have rifen already in many Places on this very Score. So that
the *Americans* remaining in the Sea-Port Towns
will have Work enough on their Hands to
maintain their Authority over their own People,
the remote Back-Settlers, or *Englifh Tartars*
(as Mr. BURKE calls them) without quarrelling
with the great maritime Powers of *Europe.* And
if

if there fhould be any naval Engagements between the new, and old Republicans on the
great Lakes of *Erie*, *Ontario*, &c. &c. me-
thinks, we here in *Britain* can have as little to
do with them in Point of national Intereft, or
Honour, as we fhould have with a Sea-fight
in the Moon, or in the Planets.

Answer 4. Granting even that the Northern Continent of *America* was to be united in
one great Empire ; and granting alfo that *that*
Empire was to become formidable by Sea ;
ftill what Reafon is there to think, that this
new maritine Power would have any Induce-
ment either of Intereft, or Ambition to quarrel with *Great-Britain ?* If Conqueft was to
be their Object, they furely would never
think of invading and conquering *Great-Britain*, fo far diftant from them ; [a wild Scheme
not only difficult, but morally impoffible]---
efpecially confidering, that they would have
fuch inviting Objects nearer at Hand in *South-
America*, and infinitely more eafy to be fub-
dued. But if their Aims were only to be
directed towards the Extention and Protection of their Trade and Navigation ; they
certainly would wifh to keep well with *Great-
Britain*, their beft Cuftomer in Peace, and their
moft dangerous Enemy in War.

OBJECTION

OBJECTION IV.

WILL not the prefent War, now carried on with fo much Rancour and Animofity, prevent the *Englifh* and the *Americans* from trading with each other in Cafe of a Separation.

ANSWER 1. IF there be any Force in this Objection, the fooner a Separation fhall take Place, the better; for nothing fhort of this can be a radical Cure. Suppofe, for Inftance, that the *Britifh* Legiflature had yielded to the late Demands of the *American* Congrefs, before they openly declared for abfolute Independence: That is, fuppofe they had granted, that the *Americans* fhould always enjoy the Rights, Privileges, and Protections of *Englifhmen*, without being *obliged* to contribute a Farthing towards the general Expence:— In that Cafe the whole *Britifh* Nation would have been highly and juftly incenfed againft the Authors of fuch an infamous Conceffion,—a Conceffion, which would in Fact have made *America* the *Sovereign*, and *Great-Britain* the *fubject* and *tributary* State. And then even the Mock-Patriots themfelves would have changed their Notes, would have exclaimed

,exclaimed againſt wicked Miniſters for betray-
ing their Country to the ungrateful, rebel *Americans*, and have clamoured for Impeachments.

GRANTING on the other Hand, that the *Americans* ſubmitted to pay thoſe Quotas which the
Britiſh Parliament ſhould require for the general
Defence of the Empire;— ſtill this would be
only a pretended Submiſſion, which would laſt
no longer than while the Rod hung over them.
For as ſoon as ever an Opportunity ſhould offer,
they would immediately revolt; and then we
ſhould have the ſame Work to do over again,
with greater Difficulties, and encreaſed Expences.
Indeed the famous *American* Pamphlet, called
Common Senſe, hath put this whole Matter in ſo
ſtrong a Light, that more need not be ſaid on
the Subject.   Therefore in this ſingle Aſſertion,
tho' in very few others, I entirely agree with
the Authors, [ſuppoſed to be Dr. FRANKLIN
and Mr. ADAMS] IT IS TIME TO PART.   Nay,
every Man of every Denomination is ſo tho-
roughly convinced, that the Colonies will and
muſt become independent one Time or other,
that the only Point to be decided is,---at which
Time, or at what Juncture, can ſuch a Separation be made with the moſt Benefit, or, if you
pleaſe, with the leaſt Detriment to the Mother
Country ? And the Anſwer to this Enquiry is
very obvious,---*No Time like the Time preſent.*

ANSWER 2. In regard to the Difficulties in bringing the Merchants of each Country to Trade again with each other; let it be observed, as the univerfal Rule with Merchants and Traders of all Countries, Religions, and Languages, that felf Intereft needs no Reconciliation: For Trade is not carried on for the Sake of Friendfhip, but of Intereft. If after a Separation, the Colonifts fhall find, that they can trade to greater Advantage with us, than with others, they certainly will, not for our Sakes, but for their own. And in Times of the profoundeft Peace, and the greateft Harmony, they never acted on any other Principle.

INDEED it is now become evident, that it ever was, and ever will be impoffible for the Parent-State to prevent the Colonies from trading with other Countries, if there is a Profpect of trading to Advantage. As a fignal Proof of this, view the prefent State of Things:---We have now the whole Force of the Britifh Empire collected together:---We have alfo as much Affiftance as our Money can procure from foreign Powers :---All our Men of War, Frigates, and Tenders ; and moft of our Tranfport-Ships are completely armed : All of them are ftationed on the Coafts of *America*, in order to prevent the Colonifts from carrying on any Trade of *any*

Sort

Sort to our Detriment. And yet we feel to our Coft, that all is not fufficient to prevent them from trading almoft where-ever they pleafe. How then fhall we be able to reftrain their Commerce and Navigation, when this great and formidable Armament fhall be removed? [as removed it muft be in Times of Peace] and when there will not be much more than Half a Dozen Frigates [or fay, if you pleafe a Dozen] to guard a Sea-Coaft of nearly 1500 Miles? More-over, it may be afked in regard to thofe very Frigates, *Quis cuftodes cuftodiet ipfos?*

Answer 3. The *Americans* themfelves furnifh a decifive Anfwer refpecting the Eafinefs of a Pacification with public Enemies, where private Intereft is concerned on the oppofite Side. For notwithftanding all their doleful Lamentations againft *Spanifh* Depredations, *Spanifh* Cruelty, and *French* Incurfions, they reconciled it to their Confciences to trade with thofe very *French* and *Spaniards*, when it was their private Intereft fo to do, during the hotteft of the War;---and even to furnifh them with Ammunition and warlike Stores for the Deftruction of the *Englifh*, their only Protectors and Benefactors in that very. War.

Answer

ANSWER 4. IT hath been found by Experience long ago, that after a Separation, even
the bittereft and moft rancorous Animofities are
foon forgot. No fooner had the *Dutch* and
Spaniards feparated peaceably from each other,
than they became mutual good Cuftomers, fre-
quenting each other's Ports in the moft friendly
Manner, and carrying on a great Trade to, reci-
procal Advantage. Nay, in a few Years afterwards, they entered into a League offenfive and
defenfive againft the *French*, their common
Enemy, and have remained very good Friends
ever fince.

ANSWER 5. THE Trade of *Great-Britain*
with the Colonies refts on a much firmer Foundation, than that of a *nominal* Subjection by
Means of *Paper* Laws and *imaginary* Reftric-
tions :---A Foundation fo very obvious, as well
as fecure, that it is furprifing it hath not been
taken Notice of in this Difpute. The Foundation, I mean, is, the Superiority of the *Britifh*
Capitals over thofe of every other Country in
the Univerfe. As a fignal Proof of this, let it
be obferved, that the *Britifh* Exporter gives long
Credit to almoft every Country, to which
he fends his Goods ; but more efpecially he
ufed to do fo to *North-America :* Yet when he
imports from other Countries, he receives no
Credit.

Credit. On the contrary, his general Cuftom is, either to advance Money beforehand, or at leaft to pay for the Goods as foon as they arrive. Hence therefore it comes to pafs, that the Trade of the World is carried on, in a great Meafure, by *Britifh* Capitals ; and whilft this Superiority fhall laft, it is morally impoffible that the Trade of the *Britifh* Nation can fuffer any very great or alarming Diminution. Now the *North-Americans*, who enjoyed this Advantage to a greater Degree than any others, by purchafing Goods of us at long Credit, and then felling the fame Goods to the *Spaniards* for ready Money, will find by Experience, that in quarrelling with the *Englifh*, they have quarrelled with their beft Friends. Let them therefore go wherever they pleafe, and try all the Nations on the Globe. When they have done, they will fuppliantly return to *Great-Britain*, and entreat to be admitted into the Number of our Cuftomers, not for ours, but for their own Sakes.

OBJECTION

OBJECTION V.

IF we fhould lofe the northern Colonies, where fhall we get Pitch and Tar, Mafts and Naval Stores for our Navy?

ANSWER 1. To what Market will the Northern Colonies fend their Pitch and Tar, their Mafts and Naval Stores, if they fhould refufe to fell them to the *Englifh?* Some Queftions are beft anfwered by their Oppofites: And it is a Fact, that were we to withdraw our Bounties, it would he an exceeding difficult Matter for the Colonies to find any vent at all for thefe Articles.

ANSWER 2. THE *French, Dutch,* and *Spaniards* have Ships, which carry Mafts, and require Pitch and Tar, Hemp, Iron, and Cordage as well as *Englifh* Ships. And happily for them, they have no Northern Colonies. Yet thefe Nations are fupplied with all thefe Articles at a moderate Price, and without Bounties. What therefore fhould prevent the *Englifh* from being fupplied from the fame Source, and on as good Terms?

ANSWER

ANSWER 3. THE *English* Navy receives much greater, and more neceffary fupplies from the Northern States of *Europe* than from the Northern Colonies of *America*. For the large, clean grained oaken Plank of three, four, five, and fix Inches in Thicknefs, fo neceffary for the very Exiftence of our capital Ships of War, is chiefly imported, and has been for upwards of 100 Years paft, from *Germany, Dantzick,* and the other Ports of the *Baltic:* The Iron (if any wanted befides our own) is brought from *Sweden* and *Ruffia*; and the Hemp almoft altogether from *Ruffia*, and its conquered Provinces. Yet we have moft abfurdly and impoliticly loaded both the Iron, and Hemp of thofe Countries with heavy, difcouraging Taxes, in order to favour the Iron and Hemp of ungrateful *America*. As to Mafts, Yards, and Deals, they may in general be purchafed cheaper in *Norway, Sweden,* and in fome Parts of *Ruffia*, Quality for Quality, than in *North-America*: Though they feldom can be rendered fo cheap at an *English* Market, on account of thofe ill-judged Bounties and Indulgencies, which were formerly granted to the Colonies; but which of courfe will be removed when we come to underftand our true Intereft.

ANSWER 4. IN refpect to the particular Articles of Pitch and Tar; be it obferved, That
originally

originally we had our Pitch and Tar from *Sweden*: But the *Swedes* were so impolitic as to lay an exorbitant Duty on the Exportation of their Pitch and Tar, presuming that the *English* could find no other Supplies. At that Juncture, had our Nation but applied to the other Northern Powers of *Europe*, they might have procured enough, and probably at a cheaper Rate; for rival Shops naturally dissolve Monopolies: But the *English*, ever anxious to favour the Colonies, tho' in the Event to their own Loss, took a different Method, by granting a most profuse Bounty to these Colonies to manufacture Pitch and Tar: Whereby they were enabled at our Expence to clear their Woods, and to bring their Lands into Culture. And after these Favours have been continued to them to this very Hour [for the Law is not yet *formally* repealed] they and their Advocates have now the Modesty to ask, What can you do without *American* Pitch and Tar?

OBJECTION

OBJECTION VI.

IN Cafe of a Separation, where fhall we get Pipe-Staves, and other Lumber for our *Weft-India* Iflands? and above all, where fhall we get Provifions?

ANSWER I. WHERE, or from whence do the *French* and *Spaniards, Dutch* and *Danes* procure Provifions, Pipe-Staves, and Lumber for their refpective *Weft-India* Settlements? The Anfwer to this Queftion will ferve for both. Now it is a Fact too notorious to be denied, that the *North-Americans* never ceafed fupplying the *French* and *Spaniards*, not only with Provifions and Lumber, but with every Article whatever, for which there was a Probability of being paid: I fay, they fupplied them even in Times of War, as well as in Times of Peace: Though indeed at both Junctures they acted illegally, and were liable to Confifcations and various other Penalties for fo doing. But what are Laws, Penalties, and Confifcations to an *American*, when put into the Scale againft prefent Gain? Even HANCOCK himfelf, the nominal Head of the Congrefs, and the Tool of artful ADAMS, was one of the greateft Smugglers on the

the whole Continent   Tell me therefore, *why* the *North-Americans*, after a peaceable Separation, will refuse to supply our Sugar Islands (whilst they supply others) if they shall be as well, or *better paid* for what they bring ? And tell me also, *when* did they supply them with any one Article whatever, without being well paid for it ?

ANSWER 2. IF the Inhabitants of the *West-India* Islands were less luxrious, and more industrious (and Necessity is not only the Mother of Invention, but also the most persuasive Encourager) they might have raised, and therefore may still raise great Quantities of most Sorts of Provisions within their own Plantations.   Consequently, if they will not raise them, they can in Reason only blame themselves.

ANSWER 3. If the *West-Indians* should find a Difficulty in supplying themselves out of their own Plantations with Flour, Bread, Biscuit, Beef, Pork, Salt-Fish, Oats, Pease, and Beans, then *Great-Britain* and *Ireland* can supply them with all these Articles in great Abundance, either from their own Stores, or from Stores imported.   And the Advantage either Way would be very great to the Mother-Country in the Increase of her Shipping and Navigation, as well as in the Extension of her Commerce.   Indeed

for

for a few Years laſt paſt *Great-Britain* hath not
raiſed either Corn or Cattle ſufficient for its own
Conſumption. But this accidental Scarcity is
no general Rule, becauſe it will be found, taking 100 Years together, that for one Year of
Scarcity, it is bleſſed with two of Plenty.

OBJECTION

OBJECTION VII.

IN Cafe of a Separation, from whence fhall we procure Rice and Tobacco?

ANSWER 1. THIS Objection turns on two Suppofitions, viz. 1. That after a Separation the *Virginians* and *Carolinians* will not fell Tobacco and Rice to *Englifh* Merchants for a good Price, and ready Money:---And, 2dly, that Tobacco and Rice can grow in no Part of the Globe, but in *Virginia* and *Carolina*. Will any Man in his Senfes dare to affirm either of thefe Things?

ANSWER 2. WITH refpect to Tobacco, almoft every Country in *Europe* can produce it in Plenty, if permitted by its refpective Legiflatures fo to do, [fee my Fourth Tract on Political and Commercial Subjects, 3d Edit. Page 205.] Nay, in *England* itfelf there were formerly confiderable Plantations, and more Ground was daily planting. But our Government forbad the Cultivation of it by fevere Penalties in feveral Acts of Parliament, in order to favour the Intereft of the Colonies.

ANSWER

Answer 3. In refpect to Rice, a great Part of the fwampy Coaft of *Guinea*, and more efpecially the Marfhes near the great Rivers, which, like the *Nile*, annually overflow, would produce Rice in great Abundance for us, if properly cultivated. For were the native Inhabitants of *Guinea* (I repeat it again, becaufe it cannot be repeated too often) to be taught and encouraged to be induftrious in their own Country, inftead of being made Slaves, and cruelly tranfported into ours, they would, beyond a Doubt, ufe and confume at leaft four Times the Quantity of *Britifh* Manufactures, more than the Slaves and their tyrannical Mafters now do. For Slaves are little better Cuftomers in any Country than fo many Head of Black Cattle; yet much more dangerous and difficult to be governed. And indeed little Induftry can be expected from any poor Wretches, who know aforehand, that a greater Exertion of Induftry on their Parts, would *only* be an Increafe of Labour, painful to themfelves, and folely beneficial to their Mafters.

[Whilst I was copying the above for the Prefs, a learned and ingenious Friend, formerly a Governor in one of our Plantations, obliged me with the following important Obfervation : " That Rice may be raifed on the Grain Coaft " of *Africa* in any Quantities: And that he " himfelf

" himſelf hath bought on the Spot, for Two
" Shillings the Hundred Weight, Rice of a
" ſuperior Goodneſs to that of *Carolina*. It
" grows on Up-Lands, tho' of the ſame Spe-
" cies with that which grows in Swamps : But
" as it receives five or ſix Months heavy Rains,
" it wants no other Supply of Moiſture. The
" Negroes underſtand very well how to raiſe it;
" but they are ignorant of the Machines for
" pounding it out : All Labour of that Kind
" being performed by Women ; and conſe-
" quently ſlow and tedious."]   Now this Piece
of Intelligence ſtrongly corroborates the *grand*
Principle, which runs thro' all my Treatiſes on
the Subject of *America*, viz. That the Coloniſts, in quarrelling with the Mother-Country,
are eſſentially hurting themſelves ; and are
greatly, tho' not intentionally benefiting us, by
obliging us to ſee and purſue our own true and
laſting Intereſts.]

OBJECTION

OBJECTION VIII.

IN Cafe of a Separation, will not the *North-Americans* fet up various Manufactures of their own, and lay heavy, difcouraging Duties on the Importation of ours?

ANSWER I. DAILY Experience proves beyond Contradiction, that we do actually fend vaft Quantities of *Britifh* Manufactures to *Spain*, to *Italy*, *Germany*, *Ruffia*, *Holland*, and even to *France* :— Though each of thefe Countries have long eftablifhed fimilar Manufactures of their own, and have laid difcouraging Duties on ours. Nay fome of them are *feemingly* fo heavy as to amount to a Prohibition. Yet, let the Manufacturers in *Birmingham*, *Manchefter*, *Norwich*, &c. &c. tell the reft. So that the Threat, that the Colonifts *may*, or *will* fet up Manufactures in Oppofition to ours, proves very little in proving too much.

ANSWER 2. THE Colonifts have already, and long before the Beginning of the prefent Troubles, fet up every Species of Manufacture, which could be attended with any Probability of Succefs :—To which End they have carried over

D *Englifh*

Englij/h Machines, working Tools, Patterns,
and Models in great Abundance: They have
alfo been feducing and kidnapping our Work-
men, Journeymen, and Artifts by every Kind
of Artifice and Pretence, for at leaft thefe 70
Years laft paft: Nay, they have publickly offered Rewards and Premiums: And have inferted thefe Advertifements in all our News-
Papers;—they have enlifted Volunteers of this
Sort by beat of Drum. I afk therefore, what
more can they poffibly do, in Cafe of a Separation?—I afk further, can they do as much? And
would it not have been *Acts of Felony* in them to
have made the like Attempts, had they been
feparated from us, and put on the fame Footing with other Nations?

ANSWER 3. IN regard to the *Capability* of
America to rival *Great-Britain* in the Cheapnefs
and Goodnefs of Manufactures (which are the
main Points to be attended to) be it obferved,
that *America* naturally labours under many capital Defects refpecting Manufactures. For in
the firft Place, it doth not abound with Wool,
or Silk, Copper, Iron, Lead, Tin, or Coals;
Articles of the utmoft Confequence in eftablifh-
ing large and extenfive Manufactures: — Se-
condly, the Climate of the greateft Part of the
Country is unfavourable to feveral Species of
Manufactures,

Manufactures, being either too cold, and too much frozen up in Winter, or too melting and fuffocating in Summer; and very frequently the fame Country or Province partakes of both Extremes. Thirdly, the Genius and Difpofition of the People are not turned towards hard and conftant Labour; a Circumftance this, which is vifible through every Part of this great Continent. Fourthly, their fmall Capitals, and Want of Credit is another very great Impediment; and it is too apparent, that this Difficulty is not likely to be removed by their prefent Conduct. Fifthly, their Defertion of the Sea Coafts, and removing in fuch Shoals up into the Country, beyond the *Alligahenny* Mountains, as they now do, or lately did, is another great Bar to the Encreafe of any Manufactures, which could come in Competition with the *Englifh* in any foreign Market. For, granting, if you pleafe, that Multitudes of manufacturing Towns and Villages are to ftart up, like Mufhrooms, on the Borders of the great Lakes, and even beyond them; ftill fuch Places, in that diftant Situation from the Sea, can no more rival us, than if they had ftarted up in the Wilds of *Tartary*, or the Deferts of *Arabia*.

Answer 4. In refpect to the heavy and difcouraging Duties which thefe little independent

Republics

Republics are to lay upon *Engliſh* Manufactures, when imported into their reſpective Territories: Enough has been ſaid already, to convince any reaſonable Inquirer, that there is but little to fear on that Head. However, as this Topic has been uſed as a Kind of Trumpet, to ſound the commercial Alarm, I ſhall therefore add, that the Situation of the Sea Coaſts of *North-America* is ſuch, that it will be morally impoſſible to prevent Smuggling, if the People ſhould be ſo inclined: And it is alſo an indiſputable Fact, that there is not a People in the Univerſe ſo addicted to a ſmuggling Way of Life, as the *Americans*. In reſpect to the Face of their Country along the Sea Side, it is interſected with large Bays, Promontories, and navigable Rivers; and full of Iſlands, and other hiding Places from one End to the other: Moreover, it is not better guarded by Land. For the Country is open between Province and Province, without narrow Paſſes or Defiles: So that it will be impoſſible to prevent an Intercourſe by Day, or by Night, if private Intereſt ſhould find its Account in maintaining ſuch an Intercourſe. But what is ſtill more, and above all, the Southern independent Republics will never conſent to prohibit the Introduction of the Manufactures of *Old England* merely for the Sake of encouraging (to their own Loſs) the Manufactures

Manufactures of *New England* (a People whom they both hate, and defpife) nor will the *New-Englanders* give a Monopoly to the Southern Provinces againft themfelves. Therefore as both will act feparately, according to their refpective local Interefts; the *Englifh* Manufactures will find an eafy Admiffion with very little, or no Obftruction. Nay, it is notorious, that at this very Juncture, when the *American* Rebels have abfolutely prohibited the direct Importation of any *Britifh* Goods, they admit, forely againft their Wills, various *Englifh* Manufactures, through the Intervention of the *Dutch*, *French*, and *Spaniards*:---But why? Becaufe they cannot do without them; and therefore muft have them even with all this additional Expence. Now, as this is a Fact, certain and indifputable, what have we to fear in Cafe of a Separation? But for a more diftinct Account, how it comes to pafs, that we have fuch an encreafing Trade, notwithftanding the Defection of the Colonies; and indeed in order to prove, contrary to the vulgar Opinion, that the Colonies never were the *real* Caufe of that Increafe, fee the Note in my Fourth Tract, P. 213---215.

OBJECTIONS

OBJECTION   IX.

WILL not a Separation from the Northern Colonies greatly decrease the Number of our Seamen ?

ANSWER 1. By the Term *our* Seamen must be meant *British* Seamen, in Contradistinction to *North-Americans*.   And then the Objection supposes, that a Separation will necessarily decrease the Shipping and Navigation belonging to the Ports of *Great-Britain* and *Ireland*.   But what Proofs are there to be brought of this ? And without *some* Proof, why must the Objection be admitted ?

ANSWER 2. THE obvious Reasoning on the Case suggests just the contrary.   For after a Separation has taken Place, the Act of Navigation will operate as effectually against the *North-Americans*, as against ·the *French*, *Hollanders*, or any other Nation.   Consequently they (the *Americans*) will no longer be permitted to be the Carriers of Sugars, Rum, Cotton, Coffee, Pimento, Mahogany, Logwood, and all other Woods and Articles for dying,

ing, &c. &c. from our own Iflands, from the *Mofquito* Shore, or the *Spanifh* Main, into *Great-Britain* or *Ireland*:—Nor will they be permitted to carry any of our Manufactures, Salt-Fifh, or Provifions, any of our Malt Liquors, Cyder, or any Wines, from *Great-Britain* or *Ireland* to the Sugar Colonies, or to any of our Settlements in any Part of the World. Judge therefore from this Enumeration of Facts certain and indifputable, on which Side would the naval Balance preponderate in Cafe of a Separation. But this is not all; for we have at leaft 150,000 Lamps burning every Winter in *Great-Britain* and *Ireland*, more than we had 60 or 70 Years ago; and their Number is every Year encreafing. Now the *North-Americans* ufed to fupply us with at leaft one Third, if not one Half of the Oil [extracted from Fifhes] ufed and confumed in thefe Lamps:—All which, together with feveral Articles depending on them, will for the future be fupplied by *Britifh* and *Irifh* Sailors. Therefore what a Nurfery is here! How growing and extenfive! And yet how little attended to, 'till the *North-Americans* obliged us, as it were, whether we would or not, to fee our own Intereft !

Answer 3. Our former Predilection for our Colonies not only caufed us to *neglect* feveral

D 4   Branches

Branches of Trade, which we ought to have *che-rished*: – But, what is ftill more extraordinary, and hardly credible, it induced us to *check*, and in fome Inftances almoft to *prohibit*, them by Means of heavy Duties. Thus for Example, we gave for many, very many Years, a moft profufe Bounty (and at one Time no lefs than 8l. Sterling per Ton) to the Importation of Hemp from *America*, as if on purpofe to nurfe up that Country into a *rival, naval* Power : But we neglected to give even the fmalleft Bounty for the Growth of Hemp in *Ireland*, as if that Branch of Trade was not worth regarding: Tho' it is evident to a Demonftration, that it ever was more our Intereft to have promoted the Culture of Hemp in *Ireland*, than in *America* ; and tho' the fertile Soil of that Ifland, particularly near the Borders of the *Shannon*, feems deftined by Nature for the Growth of that Commodity. Again, as to pofitive *Checks* and *Reftraints* by Means of heavy Duties, we have laid a Tax, not only on foreign Hemp, but alfo on foreign Iron, Pitch, and Tar: All which we ought *not* to have done; and which we ought now to undo, in order to promote our own Welfare, and to encreafe our own Shipping and Navigation, inftead of thofe of *North America*. Therefore we have at prefent the Means in our Power of treating with the Northern Potentates of *Europe* on very advan-

tageous

tageous Terms : That is, we may fignify to each of them (as we did formerly to *Portugal*) that in what Proportion foever, they will favour the Introduction of the *Englifh* Manufactures into their Territories by the Repeal or Diminution of Taxes; in the fame Proportion we will admit their Bar Iron, Hemp, Pitch, Tar, Turpentine, &c. into *Great-Britain*. Now, Reader, I afk, fuppofing thefe Meafures were purfued, what Lofs fhall we fuftain in our Breed of Seamen ? And who will be the Sufferers in Cafe of a Separation ?

Answer 4. But we have many other Refources ftill in Referve for the Increafe of Sailors, and the Encouragement of Shipping and Navigation. By the general Tenor of the prefent Corn Laws, we difcourage the Importation of Oats, Peafe, and Beans from *Ireland*, unlefs under peculiar Circumftances; though thefe are Articles which we daily want, and Articles likewife which would be fo far from interfering with---that the Importation of them, in the Event, would greatly promote the Agriculture of *Great-Britain*.—To make this Cafe plain, let it be obferved, that we might allot every Year much larger Portions of Land, than we now do [and the Land be likewife in a better State] for Wheat, for Barley, or for Barley and Clover mixt, alfo for Turneps, Vetches, Ray-Grafs, Saintfoin,

Saintfoin, Cabbages, Carrots, and other artificial
Provender and Graffes;—provided we were al-
lowed to import good Stores of Oats, Peafe,
and Beans from *Ireland* at all Times and Seafons.
And as the Culture of thefe Articles, as a Spring
Crop, would beft fuit the moift Climate of *Ireland*; fo alfo would the Culture of Wheat and
Barley be better adapted to the drier Soil of
England. In the next Place, let it be further
obferved, that all the Surplus (after our own
Confumption) whether of the Growth of *Great-
Britain* or *Ireland*, would be ready on the Spot
for Exportation to our Sugar Colonies. Not
to mention that our Live-Stock of every Kind,
and particularly of fat Cattle, might be greatly
encreafed by this additional Quantity of Food
and Nourifhment. So that we might foon be
enabled to fupply our Sugar Colonies, and all
our Out-Settlements, with moft of the Neceffa-
ries of Life in great Abundance. But, alas!
we have hitherto been fo *bewitched* with the
Notion, that we could never favour dear *America*
too much, that we have facrificed to that Idol
every Opportunity of improving the Trade and
Navigation of *Great-Britain* and *Ireland.*

ANSWER 5. THE Cafe of encreafing our
Quantity of Live-Stock is of fuch Importance
to Shipping and Navigation, as well as to all
the other Branches of Commerce, that I muft
beg

beg Leave to give it a diftinct Confideration.
I obferve then, that were a *permanent*, not a *temporary* Law to pafs for the Admiffion of Live-
Stock from every Country (which in Reafon
and good Policy ought always to be done), then
we might import vaft Quantities of Pigs and
Poultry from *France* and *Flanders*, and young
Cattle from almoft every Port in *Germany*,
Denmark, and the *Baltic*. Nay. I have been
affured by a Foreigner of Diftinction, who fpoke
from his own Knowledge, that a good Cow may
be bought in *Hungary* always for lefs than ten
Shillings, and frequently for five : And that
Droves of *Hungarian* young Cattle might be
brought to, and purchafed at *Hamburgh*, were
a conftant Intercourfe, and a ready Market
eftablifhed, for about 20s. or at moft 30s. per
Head. Allow therefore about 20s. more for
Freight and Port Charges, Rifk, Loffes, Profit, and Infurance: And then the *Englifh* Far-
mer on the Eaftern Shores of *England* might
ftock his Grounds at a much lefs Expence than
he doth at prefent: The Confequence of which
(like Water finding its Level) would foon be
felt in the Weftern, and more diftant Parts.
And the Difference between the original Price
of fuch young Cattle abroad, compared with
their Value, when grown to Maturity, and fat-
tened here at Home, would be juft fo much
clear Gains to the *Landed-Intereft* of this Kingdom.

dom.   Moreover refpecting the *Commercial*, let it be obferved, that the Hides, the Horns, the Hair, the Hoofs, nay the very Bones would be fo many additional Raw-Materials for future Manufactures   After this, it is needlefs to add, that all thefe Circumftances neceffarily tend to encreafe *Shipping* and *Navigation*.

ANSWER 6. NEVERTHELESS I will here fup-pofe, [contrary to all Reafon, and every De-gree of Probability,] that after a Separation, *Great-Britain* will fuffer fome fmall Diminution in the Number of its Sailors: Still, even on this Suppofition, improbable as it is, it doth by no Means follow, that we fhall have fewer Ships, or fewer Sailors, than we have at prefent, for the Defence of our *central* Territories, *Great-Britain* and *Ireland*.   On the contrary, when we fhall have a lefs extended Coaft to guard by almoft 1500 Miles [and this Coaft actually at *Home*, in the very Centre of our Empire, inftead of being 3000 Miles diftant from it] it is evident to common Senfe, that we fhall be better able to defend our Channel and narrow Seas with 100 Sail, great and fmall, than we could have been, to have defended both our own, and the diftant Coafts of *America*, with 150 Sail.   So much as to the comparative State of the Increafe, or Decreafe of *Britifh* Sailors, in Cafe a Separation fhould take Place.

OBJECTION

OBJECTION X.

WOULD it not be better to continue some Kind of Union with the Colonies at any Rate, rather than to throw them entirely off? Suppose both Parts of the *British* Nation, the *European* and the *American* were to remain united under one, and the same Prince, but to act as distinct and separate States, independent of each other in all other Respects; Would not even this be more desirable than a total Separation?

ANSWER I. As this Scheme of Independency respecting the Parliament, but not respecting the King, was the favourite Topic of the Congress 'till of late (when they entirely threw off the Mask, and entered into open Rebellion against both); and as the same Notion hath been advanced over and over by their Advocates here at Home, who have quoted the Case of the Electorate of *Hanover*, as an Example, and Illustration; I shall therefore examine this Matter with more Attention than it would otherwise have deserved.

HERE

HERE therefore I afk one plain, decifive Queftion,—Are *Englifhmen* and *Hanoverians* the fame People, or the fame Nation? Are they the Subjects of the fame Prince by one and the fame Title? And do *Hanoverians* enjoy any one Privilege either at Home or Abroad, belonging to the *Englifh* Nation? Certainly not: How then can thefe Cafes be pretended to be parallel? And to what Purpofe are they brought, but to perplex the Caufe, and to draw off the Attention of the Reader? To make the Cafes parallel, we are to fuppofe an *American* to be as much an ALIEN, and to be as incapable by Law of enjoying any Honours, Places, or Preferments in thefe Realms, as an *Hanoverian* is: We are alfo to fuppofe him excluded from all thofe commercial Benefits and Protections by Sea or Land, which are poffeffed, and have by Treaties been acquired, by the *Englifh* Government, for the *fole Ufe* of *Englifh* Subjects:—Nay, we are to fuppofe ftill further, viz. That the *Americans* never owed any Allegiance to his Majefty by Virtue of his being King of *Great-Britain*, and of the Dominions thereunto belonging;—but as being King of *America* by a feparate, diftinct, and independent Title. All this, I fay, muft be previoufly fuppofed. But alas! this is not what the Congrefs and their republican Advocates ever meant to fay, or wifhed to fuppofe.

Their

Their Bufinefs was, to play the Legerdemain of Cups and Balls with Common Senfe and Common Honefty. For when any *Englifh Benefit* was to be enjoyed, then we were gravely told, that *Americans* were as much *Englifhmen* as ourfelves, and therefore ought to be permitted to enjoy the fame Privileges and Advantages in common with us: But when any *Englifh Burthens* were to be born, or any *Englifh Taxes* to be raifed, for the Maintenance of thefe Privileges---then truly the *Americans* were no longer *Englifhmen*, but a diftinct and feparate People, who ought not to have been taxed without their own Confent.

Away ye Advocates for Treafon and Rebellion! Away with fuch Jefuitifm and Chicane! And ye pretended Patriots, either ftay and reafon at Home like fair and honeft Man; or elfe throw off your Difguife, act openly, and leave us. Go, and join your Affociates in *America*, and there be happy in your *free* and *equal* Democratic Governments. There preach up the Doctrine, that every human moral Agent is to be his own Legiflator, his own Governor, and his own Director. There maintain your *fundamental Paradox*, that no Man ought to obey any Laws, impofed upon him without his own Confent: And there alfo refufe to pay any Taxes, which

which had not received your own Approbation. The Congreſſes, both Provincial and Continental, will undoubtedly liſten with attentive Ears to theſe inſtructive Leſſons : And they will ſuffer you to ſpurn at their Authority with the ſame Impunity, that you ſpurn at ours.

Answer 2. Let us now ſuppoſe another Caſe, viz. That the *Americans* are declared by Law to be as much *Aliens* and *Foreigners*, as the *Hanoverians* are : But to be, like them, ſubject to the ſame Prince, under a ſeparate and independent Title ; What would be the Conſequence of ſuch an heterogeneous Syſtem ? Nothing ſurely very deſireable, if we can rely either on the *Experience* of what is paſt, or on *Reaſoning* as to what may come.

By Experience we learn, that our Junction with *Hanover* was far from being a Bleſſing to either Country. For it is well known that the innocent Inhabitants of that Electorate have been involved, for our Sakes, in all the Calamities of War, whilſt we ourſelves enjoyed no Sort of Advantage from their Miſery, unleſs the Laviſhing of our Blood and Treaſure in Defence of a Country not to be defended, can be called an Advantage. The Words of the *American* Pamphlet, *Common Senſe* are here very true

true, and very apropos, — " The Miseries of " *Hanover* [in the] laft War ought to warn " us againft Connections." Nay, we are farther taught by long Experience, that the Genius of the *Englifh* is peculiarly unfit to be joined with any other People, upon and equal Footing, or in a *co-ordinate State*; of which their Behaviour towards the *Scotch* and *Irifh*, as well as towards the *Hanoverians*, is too ftriking an Example to pafs unnoticed. Though indeed, properly and ftrictly fpeaking, *Scotland* is not co-ordinate, but *united* and *incorporated* with *England*, at the earneft Requeft of the *Englifh :* which Circumftance renders the daily and bitter Reproaches of the *Englifh* againft the *Scotch* ftill more inexcufable; for the *Americans* have declared, one and all, that they never will be united or incorporated with *Great Britain.* And in refpect to *Ireland*, 'till the much-wifhed-for Union can take Place, this Country is not *co-ordinate*, but a *fub-ordinate* State. For the Proofs of which, fee the Declaratory Act of 6th of GEORGE I. made to quell the Tumults excited by the factious * Writings of Mr. MOLINEUX. See alfo my Addrefs and Appeal to the Landed

---

* A further Account will be given of thefe Writings in my Anfwer to Mr. LOCK ; wherein will be explained, how far Mr. MOLINEUX himfelf practifed, or wifhed to practife, his own Doctrine.

Intereft,

Intereſt, Pages 80---84.   Now after a due Conſideration of theſe Facts, I aſk, doth Experience
and paſt Trials warrant us to ſay, that a Junction with *Hanover* is found to be of ſuch a national Advantage, that we ought to attempt the
like Plan in regard to *America ?*

BUT this is not all: For our *Reaſoning* on the
Caſe ſtill ſtrengthens the Argument againſt a
Junction with *America*.   Thus for Example,
Hanover is but a little Way off, and is indeed
but a little Country if compared to *America*;
nor can it ever be a greater: But above all, the
Maſs of the Inhabitants of that Electorate have
never been inſtructed in any Notions, as a *Rule
of Duty*, but thoſe of Submiſſion and Obedience.
Whereas *America* is an immenſe Country, the
neareſt Part of which is 3000 Miles diſtant from
Great-Britain : And the *Americans* in general
are deſcribed by their own Friends and Advocates, as ſome of the moſt litigious, turbulent,
and ungovernable People upon Earth.   [See
Mr. BURKE's Speech, and my Anſwer to it,
Pages 15—26.]

ANSWER 3. *Hanover* can never wreſt from
England the Seat of Empire; for every Thing
conſpires to prevent the very Poſſibility of ſuch
a Project : Whereas it has been the unanimous
Opinion

Opinion of the *North-Americans* for thefe 50 Years paft, that the Seat of Empire ought to to be transferred from the leffer, to the greater Country, that is, from *England* to *America*, or as Dr. Franklin *elegantly* phrafed it, from the *Cock-Boat* to the *Man of War*. Moreover the famous *American* Pamphlet, *Common Senfe* (in the Compofition of which Dr Franklin and Mr. Adams are fuppofed to be principally concerned) declares it to be prepofterous, abfurd, and againft the Courfe of Nature, that a great " Continent fhould be governed by an Ifland. " In no Inftance hath Nature made the Satellite " larger than its primary Planet: And as *Eng-* " *land* and *America*, with refpect to each other, " reverfe the common Order of Nature, it is " evident they belong to different Syftems; " *England* to *Europe*, and *America* to itfelf."

OBJECTION

OBJECTION XI.

WILL not the fevering *America* from *England* have the fame Effect in our political Conftitution, as that of cutting off, or ftriking away a main Prop, a maffy Pillar, or a ftrong Buttrefs from an antient, crazy Building?

ANSWER I. METAPHORICAL Objections are beft confuted by metaphorical Replies. The *Englifh* Conftitution is by no Means *crazy* in itfelf: It is built of Materials the beft, the ftrongeft, and the moft durable of any yet difcovered in the World. Moreover it hath this peculiar Excellence, that every Part of it ftrengthens the other Parts, at the fame Time that it fupports itfelf.---*Ponderibus librata fuis*, was a juft Compliment paid it by an excellent Judge, *Monf. de Lolme*, in his admirable Treatife on the *Englifh* Conftitution. But as all Things may be impaired by Time, and more efpecially as the beft of Things may be injured by unfkilful Treatment, fo it hath happened, that ignorant Undertakers have endeavoured to repair, and perhaps, as they imagined, to decorate this goodly Fabric, by fticking many additional

tional Buildings to it, which had no real Ufe, Symmetry, or Proportion; but which have weakened the original Structure, by drawing it out of its true Perpendicular.

Answer 2. Metaphor apart:—As our Conftitution is compofed of three different Powers, the Regal, the Ariftocratical, and the Democratical; and as the Mock-Patriots and Republicans are in full Cry, that the Crown hath too much Power already by the Difpofal of fo many Places; I afk, With what Face can thefe Men oppofe a Separation, if they really think what they fay? The Places in *North-America* lately in the Difpofal of the Crown (or if you pleafe, of the Miniftry) were (great and fmall) fome Hundreds. And yet you, a ftaunch Patriot! You, who are for ever crying out, O Liberty! O my Country!) You who defire to counter-act the Influence of the Crown by legal and conftitutional Means, wifh nevertheless to retain dear *America* with all its evil Appendages of Places, Penfions, Sine-Cures, Contracts, Jobs, &c. &c. &c. What Abfurdity! What Inconfiftency is this! Surely there muft be fome *deeper* Reafon for fuch a Conduct than any that has been yet affigned.

Answer 3. The *true* Reafon is the following. As long as ever *North-America* fhall re-

E 3   main

main connected with *Great-Britain*, under any Mode whatever ; the republican Party among us will ever find an Afylum for fheltering themfelves under that Connection.   This is the true Secret : *Et hinc illæ lacrymæ.*   They, good Men, are only pleading the Caufe of injured Innocence : " They mean no Harm to the King,
" or the Conftitution : They only wifh to in-
" ftruct you in the firft Rudiments of Govern-
" ment, and to trace out for your Ufe and Be-
" nefit the Origin of civil Society.   And alas !
" it is for Want of this Knowledge, that you
" are now making cruel War on your Bre-
" thren in *America.*"

Hear then fome of thefe kind, benevolent Inftructions : And from them judge of the Nature and Tendency of the reft.

* " In Countries where *every* Member of the
" Society enjoys an equal Power of arriving at
" the *fupreme Offices*, and confequently of *di-*
" *recting* the Strength and Sentiments of the
                                                " whole

---

* Dr. Priestly's Effay on the firft Principles of Government, 2d Edit. Pages 11 and 12.   The judicious Reader will here obferve, once for all, that what is inferted between Crotchets [ ] in the Quotations from this Author, and from others, is added, in order to clear up the *defigned* Ambiguity of the refpective Authors in fome Places, and to fix and afcertain their *true* and *practical* Meaning in others :

" whole Community, there is a State of the
" *moſt perfect* political Liberty. On the other
" Hand, in Countries, where a Man is by his
" *Birth*, or *Fortune excluded* from theſe Offices,
" or from a Power of voting for proper Perſons
" to fill them : That Man, whatever be the
" Form of Government, or whatever civil Li-
" berty, or Power over his own Actions he may
" have, has no Power over thoſe of another,
" he has *no Share in the Government*, and there-
" fore has *no political Liberty at all*.

" IT may be ſaid, that no Society upon
" Earth was ever formed in the Manner repre-
" preſented above. I anſwer it is true ; be-
" cauſe *all Governments whatever* have been, in
" ſome Meaſure, *compulſory*, *tyrannical*, and *op-
" preſſive* in their Origin : But the Method I
" have deſcribed, viz. [that every Member
" ought to have an *equal Power* of arriving at
" the *ſupreme Offices* of the State] muſt be allow-
" ed to be the *only equitable and fair Method* of
" forming a Society. And ſince every Man

---

others : I ſay, their *practical* Meaning : For that is the real
Queſtion, and not what the Authors either *intended*, or *pretended* by ſuch Paſſages, or Poſitions : For this is, a diſtinct
Conſideration. The Reader therefore is to judge, what is
the *obvious* Application of ſuch Poſitions, what their *natural* Tendency, and what *moral* Effect, they muſt be ſup-
poſed to have, if made the *Rule* of human Actions.

" *retains*,

" *retains*, and can never be deprived of his na-
" tural Right (founded on a Regard to the ge-
" neral Good) of relieving himlelf from all Op-
" preffion, that is, *from every Thing that has*
" *been impofed upon him without his own Confent*,
" this muft be the *only true* and proper Founda-
" tion of all the Governments fubfifting in the
" World, and that to which the People, who
" compofe them, have an UNALIENABLE RIGHT
" to bring them back" [confequently, as all the
Governments fubfifting in the World were not
built on this the *only true* and proper Foundation ; but were *compulfory, tyrannical*, and *op-
preffive* in their Origin ; therefore the People
who compofe them, have an *unalienable Right*
to pull them down, and to inftitute others in
their ftead, according to this new Model.]

AGAIN, Pages 40---43. " The Sum of
" what has been advanced upon this Head is a
" Maxim, than which nothing is more true,
" that every Government in its original Princi-
" ples, and *antecedent* to its prefent Form, is an
" * EQUAL REPUBLIC ; and confequently, that
" every

---

* The Doctor would have been puzzled to have given a
fingle Inftance of a democratical Government having been
the firft, and antecedent to other Forms. On the contrary
all Hiftory declares, I think without a fingle Exception,
that

" every Man, when he comes to be fenfible of
" his *natural Rights*, and to *feel* his *own Impor-*
" *tance*, will confider himfelf as *fully equal* to any
" other Perfon whatfoever. The Confideration
" of *Riches* and Power, however acquired, muft
" be entirely fet afide, when we come to thefe
" firft Principles.—Whoever enjoys *Property*,
" or *Riches* in the State [whether he be King,
" Lord, or Commoner] enjoys them for the
" Good of the State, as well as for himfelf.
" And whenever thofe Powers, Riches, or
" Rights of *any Kind*, are abufed to the Injury
" of the whole, that awful and ultimate Tribu-
" nal [the People] in which every Citizen hath
" an *equal* Voice, may demand the RESIGNATION
" of them. And ☞ in Circumftances where
" *regular* Commiffions from this abufed Public
" cannot be had, EVERY MAN, who has Power,
" and who is actuated with the Sentiments of
" the Public may affume a PUBLIC CHARAC-
" TER, and bravely redrefs public Wrongs.

---

that democratical, or republican Governments were *not* the
original Forms, but were owing to fubfequent Alterations,
which arofe from Difputes between Prince and People,
Sovereigns and their Subjects. Undoubtedly democratical
Governments may prove good Inftitutions in fome Inftances; and fo may others. Why herefore the People,
that is, the Subjects of other *good* Governments, fhould have
an unalienable Right to pull them down in order to introduce the *levelling* Scheme of an *equal Republic*, or a democratical Government is a Pofition, and a Parodox fit only
for our modern Republicans to maintain.

" In

" In fuch difmal and critical Circumftances, the
" ftifled Voice of an oppreffed Country is a
" loud Call upon every Man poffeffed with a
" Spirit of Patriotifm to exert himfelf. [That
is, to deprive the prefent Poffeffors of their Property, Power, Riches, or Rights of *any Kind*, or
however acquired; and even to deprive them of
Life itfelf; if this felf-erected Patriot, Legiflator, Judge, and Executioner fhould happen to
think, that the public Good requires him fo to
do: I fay, *even of Life itfelf*; for the whole Bufinefs of the Treatife is to prove, that *Killing* in
fuch Cafes is a *meritorious Act*.]

Thus far the celebrated Dr. Priestly:—
In relation to whom I fhall add no more at prefent, than juft to obferve, that this is the very
Treatife which Dr. Price fo often quotes, call-
ing the Author an excellent Writer: And that
it was circulated about with uncommon Induftry and Ardor, when the Republicans, and
Mock-Patriots attempted to raife a Ferment
throughout the Nation for addreffing the King
to diffolve the Parliament. But his M——
(God for ever blefs him) like another Fabius
Maximus,---Cunctando restituit rem.

Let us now hear another of thefe fage En-
lighteners of modern Times; who pronounces
his

his Oracles in the following Strain, in a little Tract, entituled, '' An Addrefs to Proteftant "Diffenters of all Denominations on the ap- "proaching Election of Members of Parlia- "ment with refpect to the State of public Li- "berty in general, and of *American* Affairs in "particular, printed for J. JOHNSON, Price "2d, or 50 Copies for 5s." At Pages 8 and 9 of this Performance, fo replete with Inftruction, the Author is pleafed to tell us, that "The "Hope of Mankind, who have *fo long been de-* "*bafed and trampled upon* by Forms of *unequal* "Government, is, that this horrible Evil [of "unequal Government] may find its own *An-* "*tidote* and *Cure*. KINGS being always worfe "educated than other Men, the Race of them "may be expected to degenerate 'till they be "little better than IDEOTS, as is the Cafe already "with feveral of them *needlefs to be named :* "And it is faid, will be the Cafe with others, "when the prefent reigning Princes fhall be no "more : Whilft thofe who are not the Objects "of *Contempt*, will be the Objects of *Hatred* "and *Execration*.

"IN this Situation [where fome Kings are "Ideots, and others Tyrants] the Temptation "to Men to affert their natural Rights [the "Rights of *equal* Government] and to *feize* the "invaluable

" invaluable Bleſſings of Freedom *will be* very
" great: And it may be hoped, that *enlightened*
" as the World now is [by ſuch republican
" Writers] with reſpect to the Theory of Go-
" vernment, and taught by the Experience of
" ſo many paſt Ages, they will no more ſuffer
" themſelves to be transferred, like the live
" Stock of a Farm from one worn out Royal
" Line to another [as was the Caſe when the
" preſent Royal Family came to the Throne on
" the Demiſe of Queen ANN,] but eſtabliſh
" every where [in *England*, as well as in *Ame-*
" *rica*] Forms of *free* and *equal* Government:
" By which, at an infinitely leſs Expence, than
" they are now at, to be *oppreſſed* and *abuſed* [by
" the *Hanover* Succeſſion, and the preſent Go-
" vernment] every Man may be ſecured in the
" Enjoyment of as much of his natural Rights
" [which he doth not now enjoy in *England*] as
" is conſiſtent with the Good of the whole
" Community. If this ſhould ever be the Caſe,
" even the paſt Uſurpations of the Pope will not
" excite more Aſtoniſhment and Indignation,
" than the preſent *diſgraceful* Subjection of the
" *many to the few* in civil Reſpects."

READER, what a Pity it is, that this bright
Luminary, and grand Diſpenſer of political
Knowledge, ſhould have ſo long concealed his
Name!

Name! But *Bashfulness* and *Self-Diffidence* are
the Companions of great Minds. However,
that the grateful Public may know, at least in
Part, to whom they are so much indebted, I
think, I can venture to say, that a * *young* and
modest dissenting Minister of sprightly Parts, is
the Author of this, and of several other *po-
lemical* Tracts against both Church, and State,
all written in the same gentle Strain, and with

---

* It is remarkable, that the younger Dissenters of all
Denominations, both Clergy and Laiety, are [I do not say
universally but] *too generally* tainted with levelling republican Principles respecting the *State*, and with various wild
Heterodoxies in Point of *Religion.* The Elder, the more experienced, and those, who are in every Sense the wiser, and
better Part of them greatly lament this general Defection
in their Brethren; and as they do all that can be expected from Men in their Stations to prevent it, they ought not
to be involved in one common Censure; it being but just
to make a Distinction between the *Innocent*, and the *Guilty.*
More-over it ought to be further observed, that the whole
Church of *Scotland*, whether Presbyterian, or Episcopalian,
have no other Contest at present respecting the State, than
which of them shall manifest the greatest Zeal for his Majesty's Service in a rational conformity to the Principles of
our excellent Constitution. Common Justice seems to require that such a Remark should be made at the present
Juncture, when the united Pack of false Patriots, and republican Bigots are in full Cry against the *Scotch* Nation.
And I will add further, that this is not the Remark of a
Scotchman, or even of one, who has any particular Interest,
Alliance, or Connection with any of the Natives of that
Country: But of a Person totally indifferent, who never has
received, and according to all human Probability, never
can receive any personal Advantage from them.

the

the fame Regard to *Truth* and *Decency*.   I will
alfo add, as a *Matter of Fact*, that many Thou-
fands of this little Tract were difperfed gratis
by the Republican Junto at the Approach of
the laft general Election, in order to ferve the
good old Caufe : And that it had a furprizing
Influence on the lower Clafs of Voters in the
City of *Briftol,* in turning out their former
Members, and in electing the prefent:—The
prefent I fay, of whofe private Virtues, and
public Services I muft be filent, *Ne nos tenues
conemur grandia.*

THE laft in Time, tho' not in Dignity, is the
republican Goliah himfelf, the great *Dr.* PRICE.
This Gentleman not content with treading in
the Steps of his Precurfors, plainly hints, nay
in effect *declares,* that *Englifhmen,* as well as
Americans ought to rife up in Arms, at the prefent critical Juncture, in order to obtain more
Liberty, and a better Conftitution.   For after
having mentioned in the preceding, what he
frequently afterwards repeats in the fubfequent
Pages, that the *Americans* have taken up Arms,
and that they are determined never to lay them
them down, 'till the *Englifh* fhall recede from
their Demands, he adds the following Words at
page 41 of the 1ft Edition.   " Suppofe it true,
" that they [the *Americans*] are indeed contend-

                                                              " ing

" ing [by Force of Arms] for a *better* Conftitu-
" tion, and *more Liberty* than we enjoy. Ought
" this [rifing up in Arms againft the Govern-
" ment] to make us angry ? Who is there that
" doth not fee the Danger, to which this Coun-
" try is expofed for Want of *more Liberty ?* Is
" it generous, becaufe we are in a Sink [of
" Slavery] to endeavour to draw them into it ?
" Ought we not rather to wifh earneftly, that
" there may be at leaft ONE FREE COUNTRY left
" upon Earth, to which we may fly, when *
" Venality, Luxury, and Vice have completed,
" the Ruin of Liberty here ?" [But neverthelefs we need not fly even from this wicked
Country, if we could overturn the prefent tyrannical Government, and eftablifh a better,
fuch as I and my Fellow-Labourers have been
defcribing in its Stead.   And therefore we

---

* Is there no Venality, no Luxury, or Vice to be found
among Republicans and Mock-Patriots ? And are not they,
in Proportion to their Numbers, and Circumftances, at leaft
equally guilty with others in thefe Refpects ? Nay more, is
it not notorious, that where-ever they have Power, and can
act as Landlords, electioneering Managers, principal Manufacturers, Juftices of the Peace, &c. &c. They are lefs
fcrupulous than others in the Ufe of Power for the Purpofes
of undue Influence, and *Oppreffion ?*—A Man muft be ftark-
blind, who cannot fee thefe Things. In fhort (Religion
apart, they having no Religion to *cant* about) the Race of
the Sir *Hudibraffes,* and the *Ralphos* is very far from being
extinct.

ought,

ought, not only to *wish* earneftly, but alfo to *fight* earneftly, after the Example of the brave *Americans*, in order to procure more Liberty, and a better Conftitution than we now have].

And now, Reader, having given thefe Sam-ples of Republicanifm, I here lodge my folemn Appeal, whether any ftrained, any forced, or unnatural Conftruction hath been put on the Senfe and Meaning of thefe much boafted pa-triotic Writers. If there hath not, the Cafe is clear, and the Point is decided: But if there hath, it is eafy to make the fame appear by examin-ing the Contents, and fpecifying Particulars. Multitudes of Quotations might have been pro-duced from other Authors to the fame Effect: But furely thefe are fufficient : And from thefe it muft appear, that as long as ever the Conti-nent of *America* fhall remain connected with *Great-Britain*, under any Mode or Form what-ever, fo long will the Champions for *American* Republicanifm be ftirring up the People to re-bel ; and to eftablifh a *republican Tyranny*, the worft of all Tyrannies, inftead of the prefent Government, which is certainly the leaft oppref-five, the mildeft, the beft poifed, and the moft reafonable upon Earth. In a Word, nothing fhort of a total Separation, can prevent the fpreading, or can radically cure the Contagion of of Republicanifm. And this would do it; for it is hardly poffible to fuppofe, that either of thefe Writers would have dared to have gone fuch great Lengths, had it not been for the Maxim, *defendit numerus*, and that they forefaw, that the great Caufe of *America* would become *a Cloke for their Sins.* Indeed Dr. PRICE repeatedly declares in his Pamphlet, and mightily glories in it, that the Time is near at hand, when *America* and *Great-Britain* muft neceffarily feparate. If fo, Doctor, why not feparate at prefent? And what Reafon can you give for not embracing this, the moft favourable of all Opportunities? An Opportunity, which would put an End to all Wars, and even Rumours of Wars *(of this Kind)* probably for ever; which would turn our Swords into Plow-Shares, and our Spears into Pruning Hooks; and, what is ftill more, which would fave you the Trouble of writing more Panegyrics on the Bleffings of Anarchy and Confufion. " Oh, no: This is " not the *convenient* Seafon for parting: For " we cannot, we ought not, to feparate from " *America* at prefent. Whilft *America* continues " in Connection with us (it matters not what " that Connection is) it can, and will affift us " in carrying on the great and neceffary Work " of a *free* and *equal* Republic. At the worft, " it may ferve as a mafked Battery, from which

F   we

" we may, fafely, and *under Cover*, annoy
" thofe detefted Foes of the Liberties of
" Mankind, the Friends of a *Britifh*, conftitu-
" tional Monarchy. But if we fhould be fepa-
" rated, all thefe Advantages will neceffarily
" ceafe; and we fhall be deprived of the *Ame-*
" *rican* Affiftance for ever. Therefore, 'till that
" happy Period fhall arrive, we muft make the
" Caufe of *America* our own: For indeed it is
" *one and the fame Thing.*"

OBJECTION

OBJECTION XII.

IF it be right to feparate from *North-America*, will not the fame Arguments lead to prove, that it will be right to feparate from *Ireland* alfo? But can fuch a Scheme be confiftent with Common Senfe, or Common Prudence? [See a fcurrilous anonymous Tract to this Effect, printed, I think, for BECKET.]

ANSWER I. SUCH a Scheme, as here propofed, would affuredly be inconfiftent with Common Senfe, and Common Prudence: But certainly it hath no Manner of Connection with the Arguments in Favour of a Separation from *North-America*. *Ireland* is in a Manner at our own Doors, and almoft in Sight of our Coafts; whereas *America* is 3000 Miles off. To make the Cafe parallel, you muft fet *Ireland* afloat; and then if you can pufh it but 1000, inftead of 3000, Miles from our Shores, I will allow that all the former Arguments will ftand good, and be very conclufive. Nay, I will allow, that we ought to have no more Connection with *Ireland*, in Reafon and good Policy, than we have with *Sicily* or *Sardinia*, with *Madeira*, or the *Canaries*.

F 2 But

But Providence hath fixt *Ireland* to be our neareſt Neighbour; and as the Country is too ſmall to be a ſeparate, independent State of itſelf, it muſt depend either on *Great-Britain*, or on ſome other governing and protecting Power. Therefore the only proper Queſtion is, To whom, or to what Country, for its own Sake, as well as for ours, ought it to belong? And ſurely this Queſtion is ſoon anſwered.

Answer 2. Ireland is, very unluckily for the republican Faction, lugged into this Debate; for whenever they have recourſe to the Caſe of *Ireland*, they are ſure of receiving a * ſignal Overthrow. The only proper Inference to be drawn from the Defection of *North-America* is, that it ought to accelerate our Union and Incorporation with *Ireland*; leaſt the ſame malignant Spirit of Diſcord and Rebellion, which hath ſo grievouſly ſpread itſelf over the one Country, ſhould infect the other alſo; and where indeed, with Sorrow be it ſpoken, there are not wanting already a Number of noiſy Pretenders to Patriotiſm, who would run any Lengths, † aſſert

---

* See my Addreſs and Appeal, Pages 80---84.

† I have been aſſured by a Gentleman lately come from the North of *Ireland*, that the common People among the Diſſenters are there made to believe, that a certain great and

fert any Falfhoods, and would plunge their
Country into any Diftreffes, for the Sake of becoming Men of Confequence themfelves, and of
gratifying their Revenge upon others.

ANSWER 3. THE Trade from *Great-Britain*
to *Ireland*, confidered merely as a Nurfery for
Seamen to man the *Britifh* Navy, is more than
double to that from *Great-Britain* to the rebellious Provinces of *North-America*. And yet
this Trade at prefent is little better than in its
Infancy, if compared to what it might be, in
Cafe of an Union, and a thorough Incorporation. This Affertion, I know, like feveral
others which I have ventured to make, will be
looked upon at firft as very extravagant and abfurd. But be it fo, I am accuftomed to hear
my Opinions treated as Paradoxes, 'till they
have undergone a thorough Examination: And
then, they have met with a very different Fate.
The prefent Cafe is plainly this :—Divide the
whole Coaft of *Great-Britain* into four Parts
or Portions : Let the firft Divifion be from the

---

and excellent Perfonage (whofe private and public Virtues
entitle him to the Regard and Veneration of all Mankind)
is *literally* and *actually* fuch as the young Diffenting Minifter
(whom I have quoted Page 69) has reprefented him, and
that *he cannot count twenty:* And—but I forbear. In the
New-England Provinces the fame Perfonage is reprefented
as a *bigotted Papift*, and that he goes to Mafs every Day.

Land's

Land's End in *Cornwall* up to BRISTOL, and
from *Briſtol* to *Milford-Haven :* The ſecond
from *Milford-Haven* to LIVERPOOL, and from
Liverpool to *White-Haven :* The third from
White-Haven to GLASGOW, and from *Glaſgow*
to the fartheſt Port in the North of *Scotland :*
And the fourth from the North of *Scotland* all
round to LONDON, and from *London* to the
Land's End in *Cornwall* again. — Now tho' the
Ports of *Briſtol*, of *Liverpool, Glaſgow*, and *London* do [did] certainly imploy more Hands in
the *American*, than in the *Iriſh* Trade ; yet if
you will take all the intermediate Ports into the
Account, and more eſpecially the *Coal-*Ports on
the Coaſts of *Wales*, and on the North-Weſt of
England, and of *Scotland* (from all which hardly
a ſingle Ship goes to *North-America)* you will
then find, *on ſtriking the Balance*, that my Com-
putation, inſtead of being exaggerated, is greatly
deficient.   Nevertheleſs I here repeat (what I
have often ſaid, and *proved* before) it by no
means follows, that we ſhall loſe our Trade to
North-America by a Separation : Whereas it is
obvious to common Senſe, that we may *double* our Trade to *Ireland*, if we will incor-
porate with that Kingdom, and if, by removing our abſurd, prohibitory, and reſtrain-
ing Laws, we will make of both Countries,
one grand Syſtem of civil Government, and
commercial Polity.

OBJECTION

OBJECTION XIII.

IF we fhould feparate from *North-America*, what Recompence fhall we be able to make to thofe faithful *Americans*, who have fuffered for their Loyalty to the King, and their Allegiance to the *Britifh* Government?

ANSWER 1. The Continuance of the War is by no Means a likely Method of procuring a juft and adequate Compenfation for the unhappy Sufferers. For fuppofe what is *called* the beft: Suppofe we fhould fubdue the *Americans*, and compel them to accept of any Terms which we fhall pleafe to lay upon them :---Still what fhall we get? And wherein fhall either we, or even the Loyalifts be in better Circumftances? 'Tis true, we fhall take Poffeffion of a large Country; but it will be a Country almoft ruined, and deferted. For moft of the Inhabitants, mad with enthufiaftic Notions of the Bleffings of Independency, and fetting little Value on Lands, which they know are not comparable either for Goodnefs, or Healthinefs with thofe on the other Side of the *Alligahenny* Mountains, will certainly retire thither, as Mr.

BURKE

Burke before me has well obferved : Thither, I
fay, where they have Reafon to believe our regular
Troops cannot purfue them to Advantage ; and
from whence they can make daily Incurfions on
our defencelefs Frontiers.   In Refpect to the
few Inhabitants, who *will* not, or *can* not remove, their exceffive Poverty will render them
(for many Years to come) incapable of paying
fufficient Taxes even for their own Defence, much
lefs for making a full and adequate Compenfation for the Injuries they have done to others.
Now thefe Things will certainly happen, fuppofing even that we fhould prove victorious.
But on the contrary, if we fhould mifcarry at
laft (which is certainly a fuppofeable Cafe) then
we fhall be difabled, not only from compelling
the Rebels to make Reftitution of their Lands
and Houfes to the Loyalifts, but alfo from relieving them ourfelves.

Answer 2. The beft, the moft effectual,
and in the End the leaft expenfive Method
would be,   to order a fair and reafonable Efti-
mate to be made of their Loffes ; and then
to indemnify the Sufferers out of the cur-
rent Services of the Year.   A public Lottery or
two, or even a Million taken out of the Sinking
Funds, would perhaps be more fatisfactory
to the Sufferers, than any other Mode of Compenfation.

penfation. Which Sums, neverthelefs, if they fhould prevent the Cofts of but one Year's Campaign by Sea and Land, would be a great and defireable Saving of the Expence of *Blood*, and by much the cheapeft in regard to *Treafure*. But above all, we ought always to remember, that we can better fpare *Seas* of Treafure, than *Rivulets* of Blood : And that there hardly ever returns a Moiety of the Men who firft go out, fit for Service at the End of two Campaigns, even tho' there fhould not be one pitched Battle fought. Not to mention, that many of thefe Sufferers may be fully and properly indemnified, and at no Expence to the Public, by fuch Promotions in Church, or State, in the Revenue, the Army, and Navy, as their refpective Talents, Occupations, or Profeffions have rendered them fitteft for.

ANSWER 3. IF fuch Loyalifts, who are Natives of *America*, are fo in Love with the Air and Climate of that Country, that nothing lefs than a Return to it again can content them, (which feems to be the Cafe with fome of them) then even *they* may be gratified in their Wifhes, by a proper Difpofition of our Forces now on Duty in that Country. For as a great Part of the Provinces of *New-York*, *New-Jerfey*, *Penfilvania*, and *Maryland*, are at prefent open to

our

our Land Forces, and at all Times accessible by Sea; and as they are likewise the most central Provinces, whose Inhabitants are the least infected with the Madness of the Times;—it will be no difficult Matter, whilst our Fleets and Armies are on the Spot, to erect these Provinces into four separate and * independent Republics, under the immediate Protection and Guardianship of *Great-Britain*. Thither therefore the well-affected Refugees, now residing either in *Great-Britain*, or in the adjoining Colonies, might retire; and there they might receive Lands in full equivalent to all their Losses, and enjoy as much Liberty, as Men of Reason and Moderation would wish to use, and as good Men would know how to apply. And there, by peculiar Favours and Indulgencies, they might soon get wealthy. Thus likewise, in rendering *them* happy, (who were made miserable on our Account) we should consult our own national Honour in the most effectual Manner,

---

* Two of these Provinces, *Pensilvania* and *Maryland*, are proprietary Governments. But that Circumstance would be so far from being an Obstruction to the general Plan, that it would greatly favour it. For most certainly the proprietary Governors of these two Provinces would be much more desirous of being under the Protection and Guardianship of *Great-Britain*, than to be cast off, and left to the Mercy and Honesty of republican Independents.

and

and eſtabliſh our public Character on a laſting Foundation. As to their Neighbours to the North, or to the South, a greater, and a more deſerved Puniſhment could not be inflicted on them, than TO LEAVE THEM TO THEMSELVES. And then the fanatical Hypocrites on the one Side, and the Tyrants over Slaves on the other, would afford an uſeful Leſſon to Mankind.

OBJECTION

OBJECTION XIV.

WHO will dare to move in either House of Parliament for the Separation here proposed?

ANSWER I. NONE ought to move for it, but those who are convinced in their Consciences, that the Measure is in itself just and expedient, and that it evidently tends to promote our Happiness in general; and still more particularly, that it will frustrate the Design of those *machiavelian* Politicians, who have been labouring hard, and long endeavouring to over-turn the Constitution in Church and State. REAL PATRIOTS, who are persuaded of these important Truths, ought to move for a speedy Separation, but no others. As to how *many*, or how *few* there are of this Persuasion; *that* is another Question, which cannot be so easily determined, whilst there is such a Variety of Motives for a Man's concealing his Sentiments. However, one Thing is certain, that this Doctrine is making Converts every Day; and that many Persons, even of great Eminence and Distinction, avow it at present, who formerly treated it with Marks of Levity and Ridicule.

ANSWER

Answer 2. Though mere minifterial Men fhould be afraid to propofe a Separation; and tho' the Herd of *Mock-Patriots*, of *republican* Bigots, and of * *French* Penfioners, fhould declaim bitterly againft it; yet (God be thanked) we are not fo deftitute of Men of unbiaffed Principles, and of independent Fortunes, as to defpair of Succefs. The chief Misfortune is, that many who approve of the general Plan, and would heartily join in it (were it once fet on Foot by others) yet do not chufe to appear themfeves the firft in promoting it. Now, tho' great Timidity and great Caution are Qualities not amifs in fome Circumftances, and are extremely proper in others; yet in the prefent Cafe they are highly detrimental; as they afford Opportunities to the impudent, and the daring, to Men of no Principles, or of very erroneous and dangerous ones, to erect their own Syftems on the Ruin of their Country.

Answer 3. There is the lefs Reafon to defpond in this Affair, becaufe the former Prejudices are all wearing off; and, what is ftill more, becaufe every Man now plainly fees, that we fhall never be able to retain the *Americans* in

---

* See my Addrefs and Appeal, Pages 9—19.

due

due and conftitutional Subjection (even fuppofing that we conquered them in the prefent
War) but at fuch an Expence both of Men,
and Money, as would, in the Event, prove our
Ruin.

The former commercial Prejudices were,
that the *American* Trade was the only one worth
confidering, in a national View; and that our
Trafic with other Countries, efpecially with the
Nations of Europe, was hardly to be defired,
in Comparifon with this.—The Reverfe of all
which is, by Experience, proved to be the FACT.
And the Author of thefe Tracts againft the
rebel *Americans* now appears in a very different
Light in moft Men's Eyes to what he did fome
Years ago. Indeed were a little innocent Mirth
to be indulged on this Occafion, it is really di-
verting to recollect what abfurd and nonfenfical
Stuff was vented to miflead, and inflame the
People. Nay, thofe patriotic Worthies, the
News-Writers not only proclaimed the Down-
fall of the Commerce of this opulent Kingdom,
but alfo ventured to foretell that a Set of *Cice-
ronis* would appear, in a Century or two, who
(for Want of Employ) were to conduct inquifi-
tive Strangers over the Ruins of this our once
great Metropolis. " Here, Gentlemen, ftood
" *Weftminfter-Hall,* and adjoining to it was the
                                              " Parliament

" Parliament Houfe: Let us now go and view
" another famous Ruin.   Here, Gentlemen,
" was a Place called the *Royal Exchange*, where
" Merchants ufed to meet, when Merchants
" lived in this Country." Kind and inftruc-
tive! And you too, my ingenious Doctor, you,
a Writer on moral Obligation, could condefcend
to lend your affifting Hand in this good Work:
You too could think it not below your Dignity
to pronounce a Kind of funeral Oration over
the *dead Corpfe* of the Bank of *England.* Poor
Bank of *England*! Unfortunately taken cap-
tive in the *American* War, and afterwards
fcalped, and put to Death in cold Blood
by an *American* Sachem, one Dr. PRICE.
But furely, Sir, you was fadly taken in to be
made fuch a Tool, to bedaub your Fingers in
fuch dirty Work.   Your pretended grand Dif-
covery is, after all, no more than this—that when
a Man [a Corporation of Men makes no Difference, as to the Truth of the Cafe] fhall mortgage his Lands, or pledge his Perfonals for
more than they are worth, fuch Mortgage or
Pledge will *fo far* not be *valid.*—Indeed! *tuum-
ne hoc obfecro? vetus credidi.*—And if he fingly,
or the Corporation jointly, fhall divide fuch *bad*
Mortgages or Pledges into leffer, called Notes
of Hand, Bills, Bank-Bills, &c. &c. each of
thefe fmaller *bad* Mortgages or Pledges will be
proportionably

proportionably *bad* likewife. Wonderfully great and new ! And, as you faid of one of Mr. Burke's Speeches, admirable and excellent ! Go on therefore, great Sir, and continue to il-lumine our dark Minds with more Difcoveries. Go on, and prove to a Demonftration, that a Guinea, for Inftance, if it fhould be light in Weight, or of a greater Alloy than the Standard, is *fo far a bad Guinea.*

But, my kind Inftructor, while you are bu-fied in thefe *abftrufe* Inveftigations, you omitted to mention one Thing, which perhaps is the only Thing worth mentioning in this Affair, viz. That the great national Security againft be-ing over-run with Paper Money, or Paper Credit is, that no Banker's Note, not even a Note of the Bank of *England*, can be offered in Payment as a *legal Tender*. Now this you omitted to mention. But why ? Even becaufe your favourite *honeft Americans* had made a Law formerly, and have fince made a fimilar Law, declaring that Paper Money may be offered as a *legal Tender*, and that it muft be accepted, under Penalty of *Death*, as a full Difcharge. [See this iniquitous Proceeding expofed in feveral of my Tracts, and particularly in Tract V. dedicated to the Continental Congrefs.] Now Dr. Price chofe to conceal this important Circumftance. But,

But ftill fome perhaps will be apt to afk, Why is Dr. Price fo full of Wrath particularly againft the Bank of *England*? And what Part of their Conduct has ftirred up his patriotic Indignation to fuch a Degree? I will inform them by telling the *whole* Truth refpecting a certain Tranfaction, where the Doctor contents himfelf with telling a little Truth, a very little indeed, omitting every Circumftance, which would have placed the Subject in a juft and proper Light.

Ever fince the Reign of Queen Ann (and how long before cannot be afcertained) it was cuftomary with Government, when in Want, to get Money advanced by rich Individuals on the Credit of the Land and Malt Tax; which Sums were repaid, as foon as the Money arifing from thefe Taxes were received and brought into the Exchequer. This Practice was attended with bad Confequences. For firft, the Money was generally borrowed on very difadvantageous Terms; the Lenders making a Prey of the Public in Proportion as the Exigencies of the State became *more apparent*: And fecondly, if the Lenders found themfelves diftreffed for Money before the Time of Payment of the Taxes came round, which was frequently the Cafe; they ufed to fend, or carry thefe exchequer Tallies to the ALLEY in order to

G   raife

raife Money on them. This laft Circumftance
was, not only very *detrimental*, but very *difgraceful* alfo to Government. Detrimental it was,
becaufe in the Event, it enhanced the Premi-
um for Lending; and *difgraceful*, becaufe it expofed the Exigencies of the State to our Enemies abroad, and to every wanton Scribler, or malevolent Incendiary at Home. [But N. B. Dr.
Price did not chufe to utter a Syllable of all
this.] Therefore the Bank and the Miniftry
agreed, that they [the Bank] fhould advance the
Money on more moderate Terms than ever :
And that none of thefe exchequer Tallies fhould
appear at Market to be hawked about for the
future. Therefore now they are never feen in
Public, as heretofore, but being fafely locked
up in the Bank, are delivered out, and cancel-
led in Proportion as the Money is brought in.
This Account I had from a worthy Perfon, who
certainly ought to know; becaufe he is principally concerned in the Tranfaction. He is a.
Diffenter likewife, but a very different one from
the modern Stamp, and not at all infected with.
the prefent diffenting Madnefs.

However, this Lending of Money to Government, on fuch *eafy* and *honourable* Terms,
is the Offence which has incenfed Dr. Price,
and all the Patriots. And therefore they all exclaim

claim bitterly againft it. Why do the Miniftry borrow at all ? Why not ftay 'till the Taxes are received, and 'till regular Payments can be made ? Why fo lavifh of the public Treafure ? Why fo like a fpendthrift young Heir not of Age, wafting the Eftate before he is in Poffef-fion of it ? &c. &c. Doctor I will tell you : It is becaufe your whole Faction (whether you are perfonally concerned, you beft can tell) have put Government to fuch enormous Expences, by exciting the *Americans* to *rebel*, that the Mi-niftry are forced [unlefs they will adopt my Scheme] to anticipate the public Revenue, after the Manner above defcribed :---I fay, *by exciting the Americans to* REBEL : For the *Americans* themfelves declare, that they never would have gone fuch Lengths, had they not received the moft *folemn* and *ample* Affurances from your Party, that vigorous Meafures would be taken to fupport them. Therefore I affert, that the *Americans* have been *betrayed* into Rebellion by the falfe Hopes given them by their daftardly Encouragers here at Home :---And confequently that every Drop of Blood, and every Shilling of Money expended in this Quarrel, ought to be put to the Account of your Faction of *Republi-can* Bigots, and *Mock Patriots.* I do not fay in-deed, that any of you wifhed, that the *Americans* would have thrown off the Mafk fo foon, and

G 2   have

have declared with such Vehemence against all kingly Government. No, this is what you did not wish, because you wanted to have made *Tools* of them, in order to have brought your own Schemes of *more Liberty, and a better Consti-tution first to bear*. And then :---But they were too precipitate, and both of you have been disap-pointed in your Turns :---You---by their Over-Eagerness for attaining the wished-for Object of a *free* and *equal* Republic : And *they*,---by your Tardiness and Procrastination.

However, from what has been said, the intel-ligent Reader will be at no Loss in comprehend-ing the true Cause and Foundation of the Dif-pleasure of the whole Party against the Bank of *England*. And whilst I am on the Subject, I will add still one Thing more concerning Paper-Money; [the Importance of it being a sufficient Apology] viz. That Paper Money, and Copper Money have a great Affinity with each other re-specting the present Subject. For the grand Security against being over-run with Copper Money, and against being drained of our Gold and Silver by such Money, is, that Copper is no *legal Tender* of Payment, excepting to a small Amount. Therefore no Person, as he is not obliged by Law, will take much more of Copper Money than he sees convenient. Consequently

fequently Copper Money never is, and never can be poured in upon us in any alarming Quantities. But the patriotic Dean SWIFT had almoft raifed a Rebellion in *Ireland* under the like fhameful Pretence, with that which is now maintained by the patriotic Dr. PRICE, viz. That Copper Money and Paper Money will drain us of our Gold and Silver; *and, oh fad! fad! leave not a Wreck behind.* And thus it appears but too plainly, that *Mock-Patriots* in every Country, in every Age, and of every Denomination, are much the fame. Therefore to return.

As the great Cry, that our Trade is in Danger, is now proved to be a Phantom; and as it is apparent all over the Kingdom, that Trade was never brifker, (indeed too brifk to laft, for when there is fuch an exceffive Demand for Goods, as at prefent, they are never well made; and that brings on a national Difcredit) therefore the Objections againft a Separation are greatly leffened; at the fame Time, that the Difficulties and Difcouragements in carrying on this War, are found to multiply every Day. Now thefe two Circumftances, operating together, will of themfelves (not to mention other Reafons) neceffarily bring about in Time, tho' not immediately, the happy Event of a total Separation.

G 3   CONCLUSION.

CONCLUSION.

THUS I have at laſt gone through every Objection, which can be thought worthy of
Attention.   In regard to which I am more
afraid, that my judicious Readers will think I
have been unneceſſarily prolix, than that I have
omitted any material Circumſtance.   However,
as I am now taking my Leave of the Subject, I
am perſuaded, that it is better to err in the *Ex-
ceſs*, than in the *Defect*.   For by this Redun-
dancy of Anſwers, there is the leſs Pretence for
any one to ſay, that his Objections have not
been conſidered, and attended to.

As to the Treatment, which the Author has
received on this Occaſion, it is not *new* to him,
nor altogether unexpected.   In his younger
Years, he received much Ill-uſage from the
* Jacobites: He had therefore no great Reaſon

to

---

* In the Year 1745, the Year of the Rebellion, I wrote
a little Tract, which, with the Approbation, and by the
Advice of the Recorder of *Briſtol* (afterwards Judge FOSTER)
was printed, and given away in great Numbers.   The
Title

to expect much better from the *Republicans*.
Violent Extremes are frequently obferved to be-
get each other. And on the Extinction of Jacobitifm, it was perceived very early by many
difcerning Perfons, that an oppofite Error had
luxuriantly fhot up ; and that we fhould foon
have another Enemy from a different Quarter to
encounter with : An Enemy, who would prove
fo much the more dangerous, as his outward
Appearance, and Garb were much the fame
with our own, fo that he was not at firft Sight
to be diftinguifhed from us. This Obfervation
induced the late excellent Judge Foster fome-
times to fay (and I think there is a Paffage fimilar to it to be met with in his Works) " I do
" not approve of the Notion, that the Right of

Title of it was, ' A Calm Addrefs to all Parties in Religion on the fcore of the prefent Rebellion.' It was fo
well received at Court, that the Government re-printed,
and circulated it, together with the Archbifhop of *York*'s
Speech, all over the Nation. At that Juncture I was
pretty well inftructed in a very material Point, viz. What
were the Numbers and Strength of *reputed* Jacobites in
Briftol, and in the neighbouring Counties. And I have
had the Mortification to find, that not a few of thofe, who
formerly wore all the *Infignia*, and drank all the *Healths*
of Jacobitifm, now give as evident Proofs of their being
Republicans. Perverfe Infatuation ! as if there was no
Medium between *Scylla* and *Carybdis !* And that the Reverfe of Wrong is always *Right !* Dr. Price's Book is as
much in Vogue at prefent, as Dr. Sacheverel's Non-
fenfe was formerly with thefe Gentry.

" Election,

" electing, and depofing Kings fhould be made
" the Subject of daily Converfation. This Right
" is one of thofe defperate Remedies, which never
" fhould be adminiftered but in defperate Cafes;
" and therefore is not fit for vulgar Ufe, or
" common Practice. We all know, that the
" Revolution was a neceffary Work; but there
" is a wide Difference between Neceffity, and
" Wantonnefs. When therefore I hear, that
" Men are for ever inculcating the Duty of put-
" ting revolutional Principles in *Practice*, with-
" out regard to Times and Circumftances, and
" whether in Seafon, or out of Seafon; I al-
" ways fufpect, that thefe Men mean to fay,
" we wifh to over-turn the prefent Conftitution,
" and to erect a Republic in its Room!"

NAY more, this *conftitutional* Whig, and *truly
great* Lawyer had the Courage to maintain, in a
folemn and judicial Charge, the Prerogative of
the Crown in the great Affair of Preffing; notwithftanding the popular Prejudicies were fo
ftrong, and the *Mock-Patriots* fo clamorous
againft it. And when he printed his Speech, I
had the Honour of difperfing many Copies of
this *unanfwerable* Tract, as foon as printed, and
long before it was publifhed with the reft of his
Works in the Folio Edition. But I hear, that
one, or two of our *Law-Patriots* [whofe feditious,
and

and inflamatory Harangues have been regarded in *America* as the Oracles of Law] have fpoken contemptuoufly of this Performance, and have commended the *Americans* for refufing at *all Times*, as well as at prefent, to pay any Regard to Judge FOSTER's Law-Authorities. If this is the Cafe, let them fpeak out, let them publifh their Objections, and fet their Names to what they publifh.—Time will fhew the reft.

As a Clergyman, it is often objected to me, that I am a mercenary Wretch (or as Mr. BURKE was pleafed to phrafe it, a *Court Vermin*) writing for Preferment. This is very hard and cruel, after fo many folemn Declarations to the contrary. Let it therefore be obferved, that whereas I had often faid before, I would never directly, or indirectly *feek* for Preferment; I will here add, once for all, that I will never *accept* of any, even tho' offered to, and preffed upon me.

So HELP ME GOD.

HAVING now, I think, faid enough on this Subject to convince thofe, who are capable of Conviction, I fhall proceed to obferve in gene-ral, that of all Controverfies agitated in modern Times, this about the Colonies appears to have been carried on by their Friends and Advocates with

with the moſt Virulence, and with the leaſt Regard to Truth and Decency. [No bad Argument
this, in my Opinion, independently of others,
why we ſhould wiſh for a Separation, in Order
to put an End to ſuch Procedures.] As to *Decency*, indeed there was not much Ground to expect it from the *common Herd* of Mock-Patriots,
and republican Bigots, conſidering who they
are, what are their Aims and of what Materials
moſt of them are made: And ſtill leſs was the
Proſpect that they would pay a due Regard to
TRUTH. But nevertheleſs, as they have
Writers of Eminence among them, and ſuch
Writers too, who before this contagious Diſor-
der, had maintained a ſpotleſs Character; one
might have hoped for better Things from *them*.
And yet, Reader, what a falling away has there
been even in the beſt of them! Dr. PRICE himſelf not excepted!

In my Letter to Mr. BURKE (whoſe unpro-
voked Uſage compelled me to cenſure and ex-
poſe him, as I am now conſtrained to do by Dr.
PRICE) I obſerved at Page 11, " That in Pro-
" ceſs of Time the Notion, that Dominion was
" founded in Grace, grew out of Faſhion [with
" the Antinomian Fanatics of *New-England*,]
" but that the Coloniſts continued to be Repub-
" licans ſtill, only Republicans of another Com-
" plection.

" plection. They are now Mr. Locke's Difci-
" ples, who has laid down fuch Maxims in his
" Treatife on Government, that if they were to
" be executed according to the Letter, and in
" the Manner the *Americans* pretend to under-
" ftand them, they would neceffarily *unhinge* every
" Government upon Earth. I fhall at prefent
" mention only four of them." [Which I did,
quoting both Book, and Chapter from whence I
made my Extract.]

Now an open and ingenuous Opponent had
firft to fay, if he thought proper to fay any
Thing, that the *Americans* were *not* Mr. Locke's
Difciples, and to give his Reafons for that Affertion :— Or, fecondly, if he allowed them to be
his Difciples, that Mr. Locke's Pofitions were
not fo extravagant, and fo detrimental to the
Peace of Society, as I had reprefented them :—
Or, thirdly, that taking them even according to
my Quotation, they were to be juftified, and
and ought to be defended, by every true Friend
to the Rights of Mankind :---I fay, an open and
ingenuous Opponent would have adopted one
or other of thefe Modes of Proceeding; becaufe
each of them is free from the low Cunning of
Equivocation, and mental Refervation.

But what Method doth Dr. Price adopt in
this Cafe ? He adopts neither of the former;
but

but wheels about, and attacks the Dean of *Glocefter* under the Cover of ambiguous Expref-fions, capable of different Meanings;---a Manœuvre fit only for a bad Caufe! Dr. Price's Words are thefe [Page 93, 1ft Edit.] " One of the MOST VIOLENT ENEMIES of the " Colonies has pronounced them all Mr. LOCKE's " Difciples :---Glorious Title ! How fhameful it " is to make War againft them for *that* Reafon ?" Now the obvious and natural Meaning of thefe Words, and the only Meaning, in which Dr. Price wifhed that his Readers fhould under-ftand him, is, that the Perfon who had called the Colonifts Mr. LOCKE's Difciples, had like-wife recommended the making War againft them for *that* Reafon; that is, becaufe they were Mr. LOCKE's Difciples. Now, as every Tittle of this Accufation is *notorioufly falfe*; and as all my violent Enmity againft the Colonies rifes no higher than to wifh to throw them off, leaving them to themfelves, and to their own Imagina-tions,---What can Dr. Price fay to thefe Things? And how can he clear himfelf from the Guilt of being a *falfe Accufer?* I profefs, I know of no Salvo, no Subterfuge whatever. For either he muft fubmit to this Imputation, or lie under another, which, by adding Crime to Crime, and chicaning away the Meaning of the Paffages, is much worfe. And then his Defence and Vin-

dication

dication would run much in the following Strain:
" I did not mention Dr. Tucker by Name,
" therefore he needed not to have applied the
" Paſſage to himſelf." But, Sir, the Circumſtances prove, that you meant him. " Do
" they ? Why then an *Enemy* might ſignify only
" an *Adverſary*, ſuch as Dr. Tucker certainly
" is." But a *moſt violent Enemy*; what can that
ſignify ? " A *violent Enemy* may ſignify a *violent*
" *Adverſary*." Still, Sir, you cannot come off
even by the Help of this Salvo; for you add
immediately afterwards, " How ſhameful it is to
" make *War* againſt the *Americans* for being
" Mr. Locke's Diſciples;" therefore this *violent
Enemy* was likewiſe for *making War* againſt
them, according to your State of the Caſe ?
" Oh no: I had there turned the Diſcourſe by a
" Figure in Rhetoric called *Apoſtrophe*; and was
" then thinking of the bloody-minded Miniſtry,
" and not of Dr. Tucker." Bravo!—The
Order of the *Jeſuits* is now extinct: And certainly there was no Need of continuing them
any longer, even for teaching the Art of Chicane
and Equivocation, if we can find ſuch *adroit*
Profeſſors among Proteſtants themſelves. As
to the Apellation, *glorious* Title ! which Dr.
Price beſtows on all Mr. Locke's Diſciples;
ſurely it is not very conſiſtent for him, of all
Men, who diſclaims paying *any* Deference in
                                    Matters

Matters of Argument and Reafon to *any* * human Authority, when it makes againft him; yet to exult fo much on the Authority of a fingle Man, when it makes for him. But let this pafs at prefent, in Order that we may not anticipate what may further be faid on the Subject of Mr. LOCKE. Indeed it is here particularly urged, as a *diftinct* Confideration, that he was the great Friend of the Liberties of Mankind: And I am ready to allow, that fuch a Character is a *glorious Title*, when truly and eminently deferved. But a mere Affertion is no Proof. Therefore the great Queftion is ftill remaining, viz. In what Refpects did he fo eminently deferve to be ftiled the Friend of, and Champion for the Liberties of Mankind? Now 'till this can be fairly decided, furely it would be wrong to build fo high an Encomium as Dr. PRICE has done, on a mere Suppofition. In the mean Time, he muft give me Leave to mention one Circumftance, which, according to my Ideas (I will

---

* In my Letter to Dr. KIPPIS (printed for RIVINGTON) the Cafe is ftated, in what Refpects, and under what Limitations, Human Authority is admiffible in all Controverfies whatever, religious, civil, philofophical, &c. &c. And it is further fhewn, that the Church of *England* lays no other Strefs on, or further claim to, any Authority than what is perfectly agreeable to the Rules of Procedure in all the Affairs of Human Life;—and indeed *without which Degree* of it, Human Affairs could not be carried on.

not anfwer for the Doctor's) makes no fhining Part in the Character of Mr. Locke, as the Patron, Protector, and Guardian of the common Rights of all Mankind. In his fundamental Laws of the Province of *Carolina*, he lays it down as an invariable Maxim [Conftitution CX.] " That " every Freeman of *Carolina* fhall have ABSO-" LUTE POWER, AND AUTHORITY over his " Negro Slaves." And at the Conclufion of this Code of Laws, he adds thefe remarkable Words :--" Thefe Conftitutions, in Number " 120, and every Part thereof, fhall be and re-" main the *facred* and *unalterable* Form and Rule " of the Government of *Carolina* FOR EVER. " Witnefs our Hands and Seals the 1ft Day of " *March*, 1669." Such is the Language of the humane Mr. Locke! the great and glorious Affertor of the natural Rights and Liberties of Mankind.

Now I have obferved already both in this, and in former Treatifes, that Republicans in general are for leveling all Diftinctions above them, and at the fame Time for tyrannizing over thofe, whom Chance or Misfortune have placed below them. And moft undoubtedly a ftronger Proof of this Conduct could not have been given, than what is contained in the above Affertion of Mr. Locke. But here I forefee, that an Excufe, or

Apology

Apology (fuch as it is) will be attempted to be made : " Mr. Locke was then a young Man,
" as appears by the Date of this Code of Laws
" [1669] And as he lived under the Reign of a
" *Tyrannical* Stuart [Charles II.] it is no
" Wonder, that he fhould be a little tainted
" with the Vices of the Times." Well [waving at prefent the Confideration, that *to follow a Multitude to do Evil* is no juft Excufe] let us attend this great Man to the Æra of Liberty, and to the Times fubfequent to the Revolution: Nay, let us fee, what were his real Sentiments concerning Slavery in that very Treatife, which was faid to have been wrote in Defence of the Revolution : A ftrange Defence it was ! I mean his Treatife on Government. For in that very Treatife, Book 2, Chap. 7, of *political* or *civil Society*. We find the following aftonifhing Pofition. " There is another Sort of Servants,
" which by a peculiar Name we call Slaves,
" who being Captives taken in a *juft War*, are
" *by the Right of Nature*, fubjected to the ab-
" solute Dominion, and arbitrary Power
" *of their Mafters.*"

Reader, I can proceed no farther; for the Point is here decided, as far as the Judgment of Mr. Locke can decide it. [And if he has maintained Opinions in other diftant Parts of his

Book,

Book, which *seem* to contradict this Position, I am not to be answerable for his *seeming* Contradiction.] Nothing therefore now remains, but to determine, whether this, or any other War carried, or to be carried on, is *just*, or *unjust*. And two Sets of Casuists will always make quick Dispatch with that Matter: Our *Guiney* Captains in one Instance, and such Party-Writers as Dr. Price in the other. Indeed Dr. Price has already determined, that the War on the Part of the *Americans* is *merely defensive*, consequently *just* and *necessary*. Therefore it must follow according to the above Position of Mr. Locke, that every *Englishman* taken Prisoner in the present War, is by the *Right of Nature, to be subject to the absolute Dominion and arbitrary Power of his* American *Master*. And as to the *Guiney* Captains, they too can easily find as good an Apology as the Doctor's, for making War upon the poor Negroes, or for causing others to make War against them, in order to procure Slaves. Consequently, Blacks, or Whites, the Inhabitants of *Africa*, or of *Great-Britain* are, according to this comfortable Interpretation of the Law of Nature, and the Rights of Conquest, under the same Condemnation: And nothing but *Force* is wanting to justify the *selling us all for Slaves.* Glorious Titles these! Glorious

H   Deeds!

Deeds! All the antient Republicans, *Romans*, *Athenians*, *Spartans*, &c. &c. reafoned, and acted exactly after the fame Manner.

POSTSCRIPT.

POSTSCRIPT

THE foregoing Treatise was finished, and a great Part sent to the Press, before the News arrived of the Success of his Majesty's Forces against the *American* Rebels. Probably this Circumstance may make a great Alteration in some Men's Minds, respecting the Necessity or Expediency of a total Separation. But, alas! arguing from mere Contingencies and the Chance of War, is at best a very precarious Method, and is the more fatally delusive, as it is so flattering to human Vanity. Indeed it has no Weight at all, if put in the Balance against the natural, and therefore in the End the *necessary* Course of Things. It was certainly as much the Interest of the *English* Nation to have abandoned *France*, immediately after the shining Victories of *Agincourt* and *Cressy*, as ever it was either before, or since. But, alas! who is so wise and prudent as to make Cessions immediately, after having gained a Victory, or made a Conquest?

THE only proper Inference to be drawn from our present Success is, to terminate the War

with

with more Speed, and with greater Reputation. It is now wholely in our Power to provide proper Settlements for the loyal Part of the *Americans* in the four central Provinces [fee Pages 81--83.] of *New-York*, *New-Jerfey*, *Maryland*, and *Penfilvania*; which Provifion and Settlements perhaps it may not be in our Power to make fome Years hence, or after a Reverfe of Fortune. Therefore we ought to embrace the prefent Opportunity 'e're it be loft;—and con-clude the War. National Intereft, national Honour, good Policy, and the Principles of permanent, extenfive Commerce all unite in this Point.

A

A

S U M M A R Y

O F   T H E

C O N T E N T S.

The P R E F A C E.

H 3   The

C O N T E N T S.

I N T R O D U C T I O N.

POPULAR OBJECTIONS *againſt a*
SEPARATION *anſwered.*

C O N T E N T S.

H 4   all

CONTENTS.

CONCLUSION.

A

CONTENTS.

Lately

Lately published by the same Author,

Tracts Political and Commercial.

1. A Solution of the important Question, Whether a poor Country, where raw Materials and Provisions are cheap, and Wages low, can supplant the Trade of a rich, manufacturing Country, where raw Materials and Provisions are dear, and the Price of Labour high.

2. The Case of going to War for the Sake of Trade considered in a new Light.

3. A Letter from a Merchant in London to his Nephew in *America*, concerning the late, and present Disturbances in the Colonies.

4. The true Interest of *Great Britain* set forth in regard to the Colonies; and the only Means of living in Peace and Harmony with them; proved and illustrated by five different Schemes.

5. The respective Pleas and Arguments of the Mother Country, and of the Colonies distinctly set forth; and the Impossibility of a Compromise of Differences, or a mutual Concession of Rights plainly demonstrated; with a prefatory Epistle to the Plenipotentiaries of the Congress.

6. A Letter to EDMUND BURKE, Esq; in Answer to his printed Speech of *March* 22, 1775. Wherein it is shewn, that all the Arguments advanced in his Speech, absolutely conclude for a total Separation.

7. An humble Address and earnest Appeal to the Landed Interest of *Great Britain* and *Ireland* respecting our present Disputes with the rebellious Colonies.

Printed for CADELL.

Tracts

Tracts Theological and Polemical,

By the same Author.

1. An Apology for the Church of *England*, occasioned by a Petition to Parliament for abolishing all Subscriptions and Tests of Doctrine.

2. Two Letters to the Rev. Dr KIPPIS: The 1st concerning Church-Authority in Matters of Faith and Doctrine : And the 2d concerning the original Doctrine of the Church of *England* respecting Calvinism ; wherein a Delineation is exhibited of the five Points, or of the famous quinquarticular Controversy, Paragraph by Paragraph ; with Extracts from the Liturgy of the Church of *England* ranged under each Head.

3. Religious Intolerance no Part of the *general* Plan either of the Mosaic, or Christian Dispensation.

4. Seventeen Sermons on some of the most important Points of natural and revealed Religion : To which is added an Appendix containing a brief, and dispassionate View of the several Difficulties respectively attending the Orthodox, Arian, and Socinian Systems in regard to the Holy Trinity.

Printed for RIVINGTON.

To be published, if found necessary, during the present Sessions of Parliament.

A Tract concerning the Possessions, and Residence of the Clergy of the Church of *England:* Containing,

1. An Apology for their temporal Possessions ; and a Comparison between their present Wealth, and that of any other respectable Order of Men in the State at present.

2. Animadversions

2. Animadverſions on the late Attempt to deprive the Clergy of ſome Part of theſe Poſſeſſions, by Means of a Nullum Tempus Bill.

3. Animadverſions on an Attempt now forming to deprive them of ſtill more, by Means of a Bill lately preſented to the Grand Juries throughout the Kingdom, for compelling the Clergy to accept of ſuch Compenſations in Lieu of Tithes, as Perſons intereſted in the Payment of Tithes ſhall dictate to them : Together with a Parody on ſome Parts of the ſaid Bill, reſpecting the Caſe of Landlords and Tenants, according to the modern Doctrine of the natural Equality of Mankind, and of a free and equal Republic.

4. A Propoſal for the *gradual* Abolition of Tithes to the mutual Satisfaction of Incumbent and Pariſhioners, by a Bill to *enable*, but not to *compel*, the Parties concerned to exchange Tithes for Lands.

5. Commendations beſtowed on the truly pious, and really patriotic Deſign of a Bill now depending, to enable the poorer Clergy to rebuild and improve their Parſonage Houſes, Out-Houſes, &c.; wherein will be pointed out certain Omiſſions and Imperfections in the ſaid Bill; and a Method ſuggeſted for the more effectually anſwering the good Intent of the Framers of that Bill, without mortgaging the Living, for the Repairs or Rebuilding of the Parſonage Houſe, &c.

To be publiſhed after a Pacification with the Colonies.

A Confutation of ſome Parts of Mr. LOCKE's Treatiſe on the true Origin, Extent, and End of Civil Government : Wherein the following Poſitions of Mr. LOCKE and his Followers will be particularly conſidered, and examined.

1. That

1. That every Man in Society either is, or ought to be, his own Legiflator, his own Governor, and his own Director.

2. That all Taxes whatfoever [even thofe which are for the neceffary Support of the State, and for the Payment of its Debts] ought to be confidered as mere Free-G fts, and voluntary Donations.

3. That in the Affairs of Taxation and Legiflation, if any Perfon can have a Right to tax another, or to make Laws to bind him, without his own Confent, in *fome* Degree, he muft have a Right to tax and bind him in *all* Degrees: Or in other Words, that there can be no Medium found out between *difc etionary Power*---and *a bitrary Power*; they being fynonimous Terms.

4. That the Enjoyment of Protection, and of all the Benefits of a focial State, doth not oblige any Man to obey that State any longer than he pleafes; unlefs he has bound himfelf by a fpecial Covenant fo to do.

5. That length of Time, quiet Poffeffion, and peaceable Enjoyment can give no Right or Title to any Government founded originally on Force, and not on Confent.

To be publifhed the laft of all, if Divine Providence fhould vouchfafe Life and Health to the Author.

A Revifal of the Common Prayer, agreeably to the Principles of Orthodoxy: Or an Effay towards improving our Forms of public Worfhip, without injuring, or undermining our Public, eftablifhed, national Religion.---Which Treatife will confift of the following Particulars.

1. A

1. A new Set of *firſt* Leſſons ; whereby the more inſtructive Parts of the old Teſtament will be more frequently read, and the lefs inſtructive omitted.

2. The Book of Pſalms abridged, and methodized under certain Heads of Devo ion, and Morals : The Abridgment to conſiſt of 14 Hymns for Morning and Evening Service, fuited to the ſeven Days of the Week; with an introductory Hymn to be conſtantly uſed.

3. A Retrenchment of Redundancies and Repetitions. And a Reduction of all the Services to a Length and Size more ſuitable to the Circumſtances of a public Congregation.

4. An Amputation of ſome offenſive Paſſages, and incautious Expreſſions.

5. An Addition of a few Collects to be made for particular Occaſions, the Catechiſm to be enlarge i, and the Comminatioh-ſervice to be altered.

6. A new Set of Collects to precede the Epiſtles and Gofpels, more ſuitable to thoſe Portions of Scripture, than the preſent are. N B. This Collection will chiefly conſiſt of thoſe Collects, which Biſhop [then D an] PATRIC preſented to the Rev. and Right Rev. the Commiſſioners appointed Anno. 1689, by King WILLIAM and Queen MARY for the Reviſal and Improvement of the Common Prayer.

The Whole to be uſhered in by a preliminary Diſcourſe, containing, 1. A ſhort Account of Liturgies in general, and of the Forms principally in Uſe in *England* before the Reformation.

2dly. A Stricture on the Errors of Dr. CLARK in his pretended Emendations of the Common Prayer: And,

3dly. Some Obſervations on the imperfect Plan, as far as it can be traced, of the Rev. and Right Rev. the Commissioners

miffioners appointed Anno. 1689. And on the imperfect Execution of that Plan, before the Affembly broke
up.

*Such Perfons, who approve of the Defign, as above fet
forth, and wifh to promote the Execution of it, are humbly
requefted to honour the Author with their kind Helps and Af-
fiftances.---The Favour fhall be refpectfully acknowledged;
and their Names faithfully concealed, if required.*